The Asian Texans

TEXANS ALL

A Series from
the Institute of Texan Cultures
Sara R. Massey, General Editor

The Asian Texans

Marilyn Dell Brady

TEXAS A&M UNIVERSITY PRESS COLLEGE STATION

First edition

The Ellwood Foundation, Houston, Texas, provided funding support for the reserch and writing of this book.

The paper used in this book meets the minimum requirements of the American National Standard for Permanence of Paper for Printed Library Materials, z39.48–1984.
Binding materials have been chosen for durability.

∞

Illustrations on the title page and chapter heads are details from the map by Jack Jackson found on page 4.

LIBRARY OF CONGRESS CATALOGING-IN-PUBLICATION DATA

Brady, Marilyn Dell.
The Asian Texans / Marilyn Dell Brady.—1st ed.
p. cm.—(Texans all)
Includes bibliographical references and index.
ISBN 1-58544-311-5 (cloth : alk. paper)—
ISBN 1-58544-312-3 (pbk. : alk. paper)
1. Asian Americans—Texas—History. 2. Asian Americans—Texas—Social life and customs. 3. Immigrants—Texas—History. 4. Texas—Ethnic relations. 5. Texas—Emigration and immigration—History. 6. Asia—Emigration and immigration—History. I. University of Texas Institute of Texan Cultures at San Antonio. II. Title. III. Series.
F395.A75B73 2004
976.4'00495—dc22 2003016358

Contents

Illustrations

Foreword

The Institute of Texan Cultures opened in 1968 with exhibits depicting the cultural groups that settled early Texas. The exhibit displays resulted from a massive research effort by many young scholars into the history of Texas. This research served as the basis for writing what became known as "the ethnic pamphlet series." The series included pamphlets devoted to the Swiss Texans, the Norwegian Texans, the Native American Texans, the Mexican Texans, the Greek Texans, the Spanish Texans, the African American Texans, the Chinese Texans, and many more. Some years later several books about additional cultural groups were produced, including the Japanese Texans, the Irish Texans, the Polish Texans, and numerous others.

Thirty years later, as staff reviewed the early pamphlets, they realized that although the material remained accurate, it was time for a revision of the series, along with a fresh look. Thus emerged the new book set, Texans All. Organized by world regions, each volume summarizes and provides examples of the social and cultural contributions made by the major groups immigrating to Texas as opposed to the traditional historical chronologies that focused on politics, wars, and great men. The book set includes the five distinctive cultural groups that already existed in Texas prior to its statehood or that came to Texas in the early twentieth century: *The Indian Texans, The Mexican Texans, The European Texans, The African Texans,* and *The Asian Texans.*

The author of each book used an organizational pattern dictated by the content. (*The Asian Texans* is organized by the order in which national groups arrived in the state, for instance.) The authors have additionally searched for primary sources to incorporate within the text, and sidebars are occasionally utilized to provide biographical or topical sketches. As the manuscripts neared completion, maps were commissioned to illustrate the settlement areas of the various cultural groups in nineteenth-century Texas. But as the various groups adapted to the land and people and new generations were born, their separate cultural identities began to merge with others, and the ethnic origins of many communities faded. With the exodus from rural communities to larger towns and cities in the early twentieth century, the unique cultural identity of rural communities further blurred.

Many of the people presented in words and photographs will be unknown, since most of the stories are about ordinary people who struggled to build a home and make a living in Texas. The majority of the more than three hundred photographs used in this book set are from the Institute of Texan Cultures Research Library's extensive photograph collection of over three million images relating to the people of Texas.

The Asian Texans, who did not arrive until the late nineteenth century, are perhaps the least well known cultural group in Texas. Little has been written about Texans of Asian decent, but the vibrancy and richness of the cultures they bring add much to our daily lives as Texans. It is with pleasure that we present this book that for the first time incorporates information about the most current Asian settlers in Texas from India, Korea, Pakistan, Laos, and Vietnam.

May your learning increase a thousandfold.

Sara R. Massey

Asian Texans Timeline

1849	Chinese participate in California gold rush
1853	Admiral Perry arrives in Japan
1861–65	Civil War in America
1865	Chinese begin work on the railroads
1868	Meiji restoration in Japan
1870	First Chinese come to Texas building railroad
1873	Chinese sharecroppers come to Texas
1881	Chinese railroad workers arrive in El Paso
1882	First Chinese Exclusion Act
1884	Japan allows laborers to immigrate to the United States
1889	El Paso called the "Chinese Mecca of the Southwest"
1892	Extension of the Chinese Exclusion Act
1903	Saibara starts rice farm near Houston
1907–1908	Gentlemen's Agreement limits immigration of Japanese workers
1910	Japan conquers and annexes Korea
1910–1920	Mexican Revolution
1912	End of Manchu dynasty
1917	Pershing's Chinese enter United States from Mexico
1920	California Alien Land Law
1921	Pershing's Chinese permitted to remain in San Antonio
	Texas Alien Land Law
1924	Asian Exclusion Act by the U.S. Congress
1937	Japanese invade China
1941	Japanese drop bombs on Pearl Harbor
1942	Japanese Americans moved into internment camps
1943	Chinese Exclusion Act repealed by Congress
1945	End of World War II
	U.S. occupation of Japan
	Congress passes War Brides Act

1946	Philippine independence
1947	Soldiers' Brides Bill extended to all ethnic groups
	India gains independence from United Kingdom
	Pakistan is created
1949	Communist Chinese take over China
	Nationalist Chinese move to Formosa (Taiwan)
1950	United States at war in Korea
1954–75	United States involved in Vietnam War
1965	Immigration reforms allow large numbers of Asians to immigrate to U.S.
1975	Fall of Saigon and Vietnamese refugees arrive
1979	Second wave of refugees arrive from Indochina

The Asian Texans

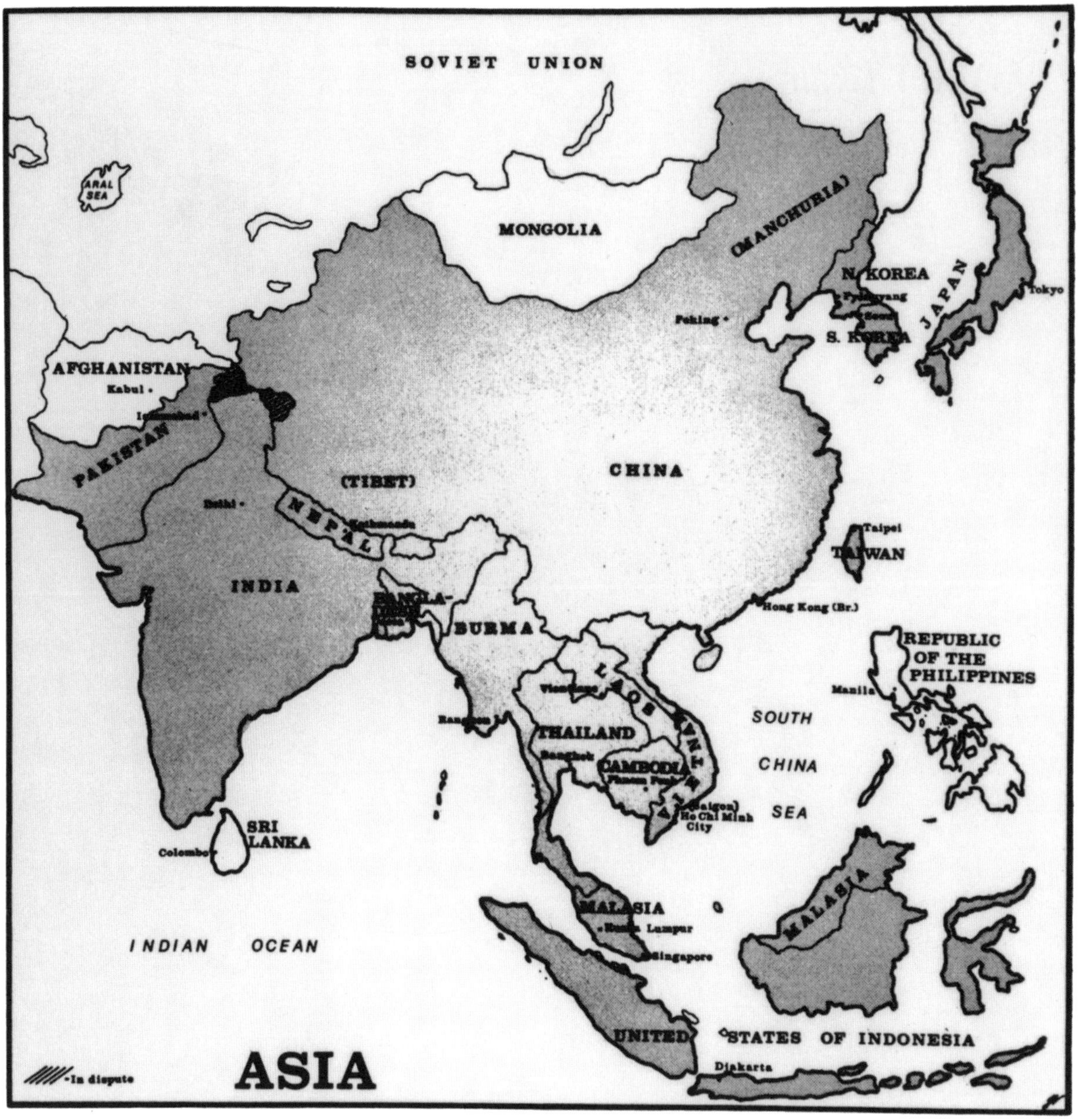

Map of Asia. From *The World of Asia* by Iriye et al. © 1979 Forum Press. Reprinted by permission from Harlan Davidson, Inc.

Introduction

ASIANS ARRIVED in Texas at different times, from different places, and under very different conditions. The major migration occurred in two waves, separated by decades in which national law prohibited Asians from entering the United States. Chinese laborers came after the Civil War to work on the railroads and in the cotton fields, and by 1900 Japanese farmers were also working in the fields of Texas.

In 1882, for the Chinese, and in 1924, for other Asians, immigration virtually ceased only to be reopened gradually during World War II. Dramatic changes in the immigration laws in 1965, and the Vietnamese refugee crisis that occurred a decade later, resulted in a wave of new Asians coming to Texas.

Worshiping and celebrating as Buddhists, Hindus, or Muslims, as Chinese, Pakistani, or Cambodian, Asians brought their home culture as they moved into their new surroundings. Despite contributions to the state's development, many Texans tended to lump all Asians together, ignoring or harassing them as "dirty heathens" and "the yellow peril." Their different physical appearance, languages, religions, and cultures threatened some Texans. Consequently, some Asians became successful in Texas only by discarding their traditions. Others found identity and comfort in preserving their cultures while affirming their loyalty to the United States.

Asia is a massive and geographically diverse continent stretching from the Pacific Ocean westward to Europe. The first Asian immigrants came to the United States from the eastern regions of China

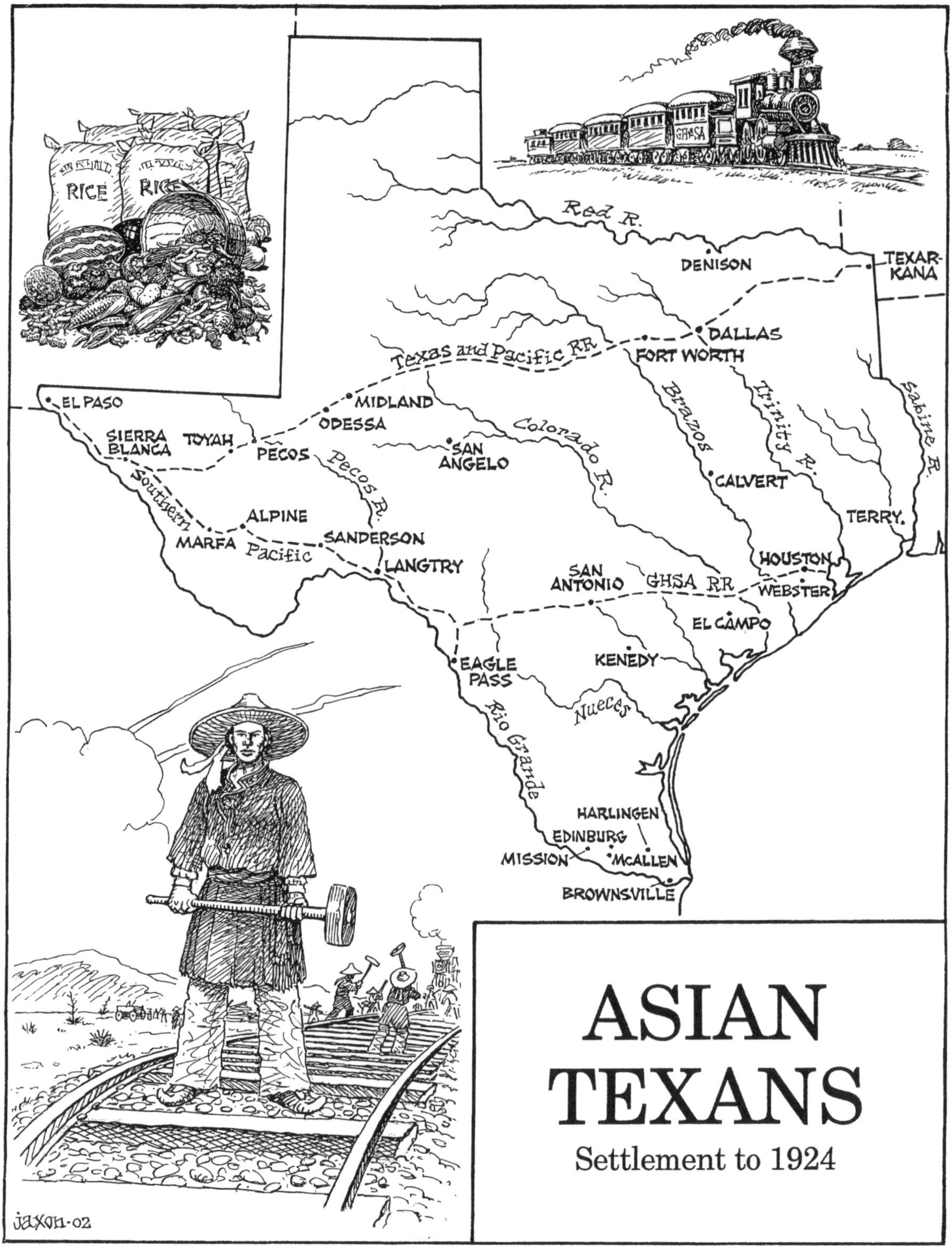

Asian Texans Settlement to 1924. Map by Jack Jackson

and Japan, along the Pacific Rim where they had encountered traders from the United States. The largest groups of the new immigrants to come to Texas in recent decades have arrived from East Asian nations such as Korea, the Philippine Islands, Vietnam, Laos, and Cambodia. Other new immigrants, arriving by plane rather than by boat, have come from India and Pakistan in South Central Asia. Smaller numbers of Asian people, not included here, came from other Asian countries.

The Asian Texans differ greatly among themselves. Distinctive physical features set them apart from each other as well as from non-Asians. Just as an Irish person might be surprised to be mistaken for a Swede, Asians resent being lumped with other Asian groups. Each Asian nation has its own distinct culture and language, and countries such as India and China have an enormous variety of cultural regions within the country. Ethnic and religious groups of Asia also have a long history of invasion and war against each other. Most individuals primarily identify with their home region within a country and with their religion rather than with the general category of Asian.

When Asians first came to Texas, the U.S. census had only two racial categories—Caucasian and colored. All people not of European descent were labeled "colored." Thus the early Chinese and Japanese, along with Native Americans, African Americans, and Latin Americans, were grouped together in the census count. Based on a law passed in 1790 during George Washington's administration, none could become U.S. citizens. National legislation, passed in 1924, stopped all legal Asian immigration. Behind the legal restrictions discriminating against Asians, real hatred and fear of them by U.S. citizens existed. Job competition caused some of the fear. Distorted information and misunderstandings about ethnic groups also raised tensions. Some politicians found that blaming the Asians for unpleasant situations helped get votes. Although Asian Texans were often treated well and respected by their neighbors, discrimination, prejudice, and even murder also occurred.

Asian cultures have blended and overlapped in ways difficult for other Texans to understand. Asian people and ideas have interacted, and national boundaries have been drawn and redrawn over the centuries. Asian thought and lifestyles share features that set them apart from those developed by the Europeans and their descendants. In most Asian religions, belief is less important than "right living." European and American concepts claiming that the mind or soul is separate from the body are not present in Asian thought. Religion is not separate from secular life but practiced daily as a path or an orientation for all life activities. Asians come together to celebrate religious festivals, but the weekly congregating on Sundays familiar to Christians is of little significance to many of them.

Asian religions have developed side by side and blended together over the centuries. Hinduism emerged first in India. Jains and Sikhs developed separate traditions alongside it. Buddhism grew out of a Hindu society before spreading throughout East Asia and developing into distinct patterns. In China, Korea, and Indochina, it merged with the social and ethical thought of Confucian and Taoist principles. In Japan, Buddhism combined with native Shinto practices. Only the Islamic religion, related to European Christianity and Judaism, rejected such religious blending.

As the Muslim Empire grew in the seventh century to include the lands of the Middle East, North Africa, and Persia, Islam spread throughout Asia into areas where Muslims still practice their faith. The Zoroastrian religion began in ancient Persia, present-day Iran, but some of its followers live in India today. Christians in India tend

TABLE 1

The Number of Religious Temples and Mosques in Texas, 2001

Buddhist	90
Muslim	38
Hindu	34
Sikh	13
Jain	6
Zoroastrian	3

Source: Internet: http://www.pluralism.org *(Nov., 2001).*

to belong to the Eastern Orthodox traditions rather than those that developed in Western Europe. Colonizers from Spain and France brought Roman Catholicism to the Philippines and Vietnam.

All major Asian religions include similar ethical or moral laws. They prohibit killing, stealing, and lying and urge followers to treat others with compassion and respect. All Asian religions and cultures also place great importance on the family as a nuclear unit of parents and children, as an extended household involving grandparents, and as a network of aunts, uncles, and cousins. Loyalty and sacrifice to this extended familial group is valued over individual gain and achievement. Parents, elders, and teachers all demand respect, and a person's shame disgraces the entire family group. The Asian culture views hard work as critical for achievement and even for the survival of the family and the group. Many recently arrived Asians believe more strongly in family closeness and work than non-Asians who have lived here for generations. In addition, Asian cultures generally stress listening over speaking and agreeing over voicing one's dissent. Texan schools and workplaces do not always value such behavior, creating confusion for some Asian Texans.

World War II dramatically increased the U.S. involvement in Asia. The aftermath of the war created new opportunities for emigration from the continent. Although Japanese Americans experienced harassment and detention in internment camps, Asians who fought beside U.S. troops gained gradual acceptance. In a slow, scattered fashion, the U.S. government began to let Asians enter the country and become citizens.

Women from Japan, China, Korea, and the Philippines married U.S. soldiers, both Asian and non-Asian, stationed in Asia in the 1940s and 1950s. As "war brides" the women were allowed to accompany their husbands back to the United States, usually settling near military bases. The first war bride legislation, passed in 1945, allowed brides from England and other European countries to come to the United States but excluded all Asian brides. The government corrected this omission in 1947 and, for the first time, immigration legislation applied to all, regardless of race or national origin.

The legal reforms of 1952 expanded Asians' rights to include U.S. citizenship and allowed a few to enter the country. While the Japanese in Texas who wanted to become citizens rejoiced, the quota system still severely limited new immigration by Asians.

In 1965 an expanding postwar economy, less rigid attitudes about race, and a sense of humanitarianism led to dramatic new immigration legislation that ended the 1924 quota system. For the first time, large numbers of Asians from many different countries could enter the United States. The new Asian immigrants were different from the early immigrants who had come prior to 1924. The new laws gave a high priority to professionals that the United States needed in fields like medicine and science. Many of the new Asian immigrants were well educated in their home countries. Others attended schools and colleges in the United States and then remained in this country. New laws encouraged families to enter the United States, and many did so in great numbers.

With the changes in immigration laws that occurred during the second half of the twentieth century, Asian immigration increased significantly. The 2000 census reported 657,664 people in Texas with one or both parents of Asian descent. As a group they continue to be an increasingly important group in Texas.

Coming from countries like India and Pakistan that previously had sent few immigrants to the United States, the new immigrants encountered a place unlike that of their predecessors. Often they spoke English and came because they were drawn to the affluent lifestyle they had learned about from the media. They kept in close contact with friends and family back home by telephone and E-mail. They returned often to visit, taking their children along to learn their cultural heritage.

Following the U.S. withdrawal from Vietnam in 1975, refugees from Indochina came to this country. Often they lacked the resources and professional skills of other new immigrants. Large numbers clustered in Texas cities where they sought to create new lives while honoring their pasts.

TABLE 2.
Asian Census Population in Texas, 2000

	Total Texas	Houston	Dallas	Fort Worth	Austin	San Antonio	Killeen	El Paso
Total Asian	657,664	245,418	160,917	62,438	51,985	32,894	10,943	9,233
Vietnamese	143,352	64,272	29,369	20,392	9,351	3,371	512	347
Asian Indian	142,689	55,011	42,852	11,123	11,837	4,610	803	1,143
Chinese	112,950	48,294	29,057	6,516	11,344	4,903	713	1,300
Filipino	75,226	24,692	12,415	4,977	3,865	7,810	2,583	1,882
Korean	54,300	11,167	16,192	3,948	5,672	4,197	4,284	2,174
Japanese	28,060	5,963	5,881	2,376	2,907	3,487	996	1,496
Pakistani	25,324	13,917	5,377	2,241	1,252	507	54	51
Laotian	11,626	1,546	3,376	4,198	273	337	47	22
Thai	9,918	2,074	2,280	1,314	1,094	1,110	370	125
Taiwanese	8,638	3,925	1,963	546	970	266	13	69
Cambodian	8,225	2,655	3,125	358	458	175	41	12

Source: Internet: http://txdoc.tamu.edu/data/census/2000 *(Nov., 2001).*

Asian Texans are selectively assimilating into society while privately retaining the cultural traditions they value. Religion remains central to their identity. As both Americans and members of their ethnic and cultural communities, they are contributing to a pluralistic Texas. Their celebrations and customs provide all Texans with a new perspective on who we are as Americans. Asian Texans can also teach other Americans how to live in a society where we share common loyalties while still celebrating our diversity.

CHAPTER 1
Chinese Texans

THE FIRST ASIANS to arrive in Texas came from China, a vast country stretching from the Pacific Ocean west into the mountainous land bordering eastern Europe. Although China was once a powerful center of culture and knowledge, by the nineteenth century it had evolved into a loosely governed kingdom. Poverty and fighting among tribal warlords was widespread. Most immigrants to the United States came from the coast of southern China, which had a history of shipbuilding, trade, and communication with foreigners.

The first Chinese who came to the United States joined the California gold rush in 1849 and stayed on as laborers. Almost all were single men or young husbands who left wives behind in China with their parents. Like many Europeans, they came hoping to earn money and eventually return to their native countries. Some achieved this goal, but others made new homes in the United States, including Texas.

After the Civil War and the end of slavery, some former slave owners hoped to use Chinese men to replace the African American workers. The first Chinese were brought from California to Texas by the Houston and Texas Central Railroad Company in 1870 to be used "in place of blacks." Nearly three hundred Chinese entered the Brazos River Valley to lay the track from Calvert, in Robertson County, toward Dallas. However, the Chinese worked for the Houston and Texas Central Railroad only a few months before leaving and becoming farm laborers.

Farmers in Robertson County made sharecropping contracts with these Chinese, again seeking to replace freed slaves. The Chinese worked long, hard hours. Initially, employers viewed them as docile, but when employers broke their contracts, did not pay on time, or demanded extra work, the Chinese simply quit.

A few Chinese settled in East Texas communities. In Calvert several of the men married African American women. Their descendants, known as "Black Chinese," remained in Robertson County until at least the 1970s. For example, Arthur Williams was the son of Bar Low, who came in 1874. Local people described him as "a little low man who had a queue, wore pajama-like suits and had very small feet."[1] Johnny Yepp was the son of Tom Yepp, who also arrived in 1874. Because Johnny's mother was black, he attended segregated schools with other blacks and later married a black woman himself. In the election of 1874, 150 Chinese in Robertson County voted.

Chinese men also arrived in Houston. In 1900, laundryman Wah Yuan opened a shop there. He and his white wife, Anna, had a four-month-old son, named Lincoln Yuan.

As construction began on the portion of the transcontinental railroad that was to cross Texas, more Chinese men arrived as laborers to lay tracks. Using as many as three thousand Chinese workers, the Texas and Pacific started building west from Texarkana and Dallas through Abilene to Toyah, where a Chinese community developed, and on toward El Paso. The Southern Pacific reached El Paso from California and continued building toward the east with two thousand Chinese employed. The two railroads met at Sierra Blanca in November, 1881. Still wanting a railroad to the Gulf, the Southern Pacific and the Galveston, Harrisburg and San Antonio Railway continued building across South Texas. Chinese made up the majority of the crews working eastward from Langtry. In January, 1883, workers connected the rail lines at "Painted Cave" near the Pecos River Bridge.

According to the *San Antonio Daily Express,* the Chinese railroad workers were "treated more like slaves than anything else," and other workers harassed them.[2] Allegedly, the graves of many Chi-

C. C. Charles was a laundryman for Emil Schuetze in Corpus Christi, Texas, ca. 1890. Institute of Texan Cultures illustration no. 76-246

An advertisement for the Galveston, Harrisburg and San Antonio Railway that began operation in 1877. Institute of Texan Cultures illustration no. 73-903

nese laborers lie along the Southern Pacific track in far West Texas towns like Marfa and Alpine.

Railroad work isolated the Chinese and allowed them to retain their lifestyle. Working in traditional loose shirts and pants and straw hats, they stayed to themselves. They worked in gangs of a dozen or more with a headman who contracted the group's work and collected their wages each evening. Cooks prepared their familiar meals with dried oysters, dried cuttlefish, dried bamboo, salted cabbage, rice, mushrooms, pork, poultry, and tea. Many of the foods were imported in bulk from California and China. While working, they drank tea from powder kegs that were transported by carrying the kegs at ends of a pole placed across their shoulders. The men slept in tents arranged in tight clusters of fifteen to thirty men and, unlike the non-Chinese workers, kept their camps very clean. The men wore their hair braided down their backs in long queues in honor of the Chinese emperor. Many Chinese cut off their traditional queues in 1911 when the Manchu dynasty was overthrown.

Artifacts discovered at the Chinese railroad camps are displayed at Seminole Canyon State Park at the mouth of the Pecos River near

Langtry. Many of the artifacts were made in China: glazed ceramic dishes, woks, stacked dish covers used in cooking, and some herbal bottles. A few products, such as an iron kettle and cloth suitcases, were made in the United States.

After workers completed the railroads across Texas, some of the men left the state while others settled into available jobs. One group of railroad workers went to San Antonio and started a small Chinese community there while others settled in San Angelo. Some continued to work for the railroad, living near the roundhouses in Toyah and El Paso. Sing Lee came to Toyah about 1880 as an eighteen-year-old to work for the railroad. He was still there in the 1950s—the last of the Chinese in Toyah. He lived in the same adobe house with Mexican rather than Chinese neighbors. He subscribed to a Chinese newspaper, which he regularly read sitting in front of the post office.

In Sanderson a group of Chinese ran a restaurant and boardinghouse where ranchers and their families stayed while their homes were under construction. North of Sanderson, Chinese built the roadway up "Big Hill." Officers' wives at Fort Davis spoke well of the Chinese who came and worked as servants for their families.

In the 1900s, El Paso had the largest Chinese community in Texas. About three hundred Chinese lived between the Rio Grande and the downtown area. Some did maintenance work on the trains, which were headquartered there, while others worked as gardeners and servants. Chinese also opened boardinghouses, barbershops, and restaurants that served their countrymen. In addition, Chinese doctors and barbers served the larger community. Mexicans living in both El Paso and Juárez shopped in the Chinese-owned stores. The whites used the Chinese laundries, much to the dismay of the Mexican women who competed for the work. Whites also patronized the Chinese opium dens and gambling houses. Chinese merchants sold products from China and served as bankers for other Chinese and as representatives to the larger community. Some Chinese leased land near El Paso for raising vegetables that they then sold in the city. The Chinese also created their own organizations, which substituted in part for their absent families. Congregating at a temple helped them to maintain their traditional religious practices.

Anti-Chinese sentiment had developed in California and other states on the Pacific Coast by the 1880s. Euro-American workers claimed that the Chinese worked for so little money that they got all the jobs. Others asserted that the Chinese were racially inferior. In 1882 and again in 1892, the U.S. government passed laws preventing additional Chinese workers from coming into the United States. Only a few merchants and their wives, students, and other privileged Chinese could immigrate. Although large numbers of Chinese men no longer came to the United States, some living in California moved to El Paso in the 1880s to escape the violence against them.

Few Chinese women lived in the United States when the Chinese Exclusion Act was passed. With the new legislation, the men lost all hope of bringing their wives to the United States. In 1900 there were 823 Chinese men in Texas but only 18 Chinese women. In El Paso there were 239 Chinese men and 4 Chinese women. Some men married Mexican women, and a few merchants managed to bring wives from China. Many Chinese men never married and sometimes attached themselves to Chinese families as "bachelor uncles." Those that could afford it maintained a wife, family, and home back in China and returned every few years to visit. Some men who left their wives in China never saw them again, although they regularly sent them money.

The Chinese in Mexico initially worked to build the railroads there, and eventually they started small businesses. While Chinese were free to immigrate to Mexico, they were not well received. Mexicans resented their aggressive, successful style of business and passed laws restricting their activities. Since Chinese workers could not enter the United States legally after 1882, some came as "illegal immigrants" from Mexico. El Paso, with its four railroads, was a popular point of entry. Residents of the city hid illegal Chinese until they could be secretly taken out of town. The ruins of a few secret rooms have been found, but no traces were uncovered of the rumored honeycomb of tunnels connecting buildings throughout the Chinese com-

A fashionable young Chinese woman, Mrs. Poy Eng. Institute of Texan Cultures illustration no. 76-447

Sam MarDock

Mar Yum Eh was born in a village near Canton, China, in 1862. At the age of thirteen, he came to the United States. He worked on farms and ranches in California, cooking and breaking horses. He was given the name Sam. When the Southern Pacific Railroad began to lay track across present-day Arizona and New Mexico, Sam joined their work crews. He had learned English and could keep accounts, and the boss made him foreman for the other Chinese as they laid track near Del Rio.

After leaving the railroad, Sam held a variety of jobs around Texas. He worked as an interpreter, sold horses, and gambled. As he earned money, he saved it and bought a restaurant in Tyler, the Grand Star Cafe. Soon he opened a second restaurant, the Cotton Belt,

munity. In 1904 the *El Paso Herald* claimed that "if Chinese immigration to Mexico continues it will be necessary to run a barbed wire along our side of the Rio Grande."[3]

Chinese also crossed the Rio Grande at other points in West Texas. Eagle Pass was a frequent point of entry. Even Pecos, about two hundred miles from the Mexican border, allegedly had homes with secret rooms where illegal Chinese hid. In West Texas, the U.S. Immigration Service rounded up groups of Chinese, along with some Japanese and Lebanese, and sent them to San Francisco for deportation. One time a railroad conductor found fourteen Chinese aliens, nearly dead from thirst, sealed in a freight car of copper ore that came from Mexico. Another story claims that in 1905 five hundred Chinese reluctantly boarded a train from Sanderson and then were killed when the train ran off the track. A major task of the U.S. border patrol, created by the 1924 Immigration Restriction Act, was to stop the illegal entry of Chinese.

CHINESE SETTLEMENT AND COMMUNITY BUILDING

Despite the ban on Chinese entry into the United States, the Chinese community in Texas continued to grow during the early 1900s. The presence of a few Chinese women scattered throughout the state meant that some Chinese children were born in Texas. Although laborers, the largest group of Chinese immigrants, were excluded, merchants obtained permission to bring in their wives. When the 1906 earthquake in San Francisco destroyed the immigration records, Chinese merchants contrived to bring in "paper sons," male relatives who would work in their businesses. Obtaining legal certification took place at Angel Island, the port of entry for Asian immigrants. After weeks of waiting and detailed questioning, officials returned many back to China.

Events of the Mexican Revolution also led to the arrival of several hundred Chinese in Texas. Because Chinese and Japanese who

Sam MarDock, his wife, and children pose before their home in Tyler, Texas.
Institute of Texan Cultures illustration no. 76-554

near the railroad track. Because the Cotton Belt had also served as a general store, Sam became a merchant, making him legally eligible to bring a wife to Texas.

In 1897 Sam returned to China and married Wong Shee. She dressed in red—a lucky color for the Chinese—and they had a traditional Chinese wedding. Living in a large house that Sam had built for her, she remained in China for fourteen years. Then Sam returned and accompanied her by boat to California. At Angel Island, she was certified to enter the United States as the wife of merchant Sam MarDock. Arriving in Tyler, she removed the foot bindings that she had worn since childhood to make her feet small, which for the Chinese was a sign of beauty.

lived in Juárez were endangered as the Mexican revolutionaries neared their city, U.S. officials allowed them to cross into El Paso when the fighting started. Leaders promised that the Asians would return to Mexico, but some Chinese remained in Texas, opening shops in El Paso or moving on to other destinations.

When the fighting in Mexico broke out, Chinese sold goods to both sides and even fought against Pancho Villa. In response, Villa publicly threatened to kill all the Chinese he could find, along with the Mexican women married to them.

In 1916 the U.S. forces under Gen. John J. Pershing entered Mexico. The army had difficulties getting supplies for the men until local Chinese began selling food and other products to them. They also set up small laundries and served as laborers at the military camps. When Pershing withdrew from Mexico in 1917, over five hundred Chinese accompanied him.

Despite laws prohibiting Chinese from entering the United States, Pershing persuaded Congress that these Chinese should be admit-

At first, Sam and Wong lived in an apartment at the Cotton Belt Restaurant and Store. They had three children. Sam prospered by owning several restaurants in Tyler, running a nearby wood yard, and raising hogs on his farm. He moved his family into a new house in a fashionable neighborhood, and the MarDock children attended public schools and college. When Sam MarDock died in 1942, he and his family had become a vital part of the East Texas town of Tyler.

Source: Julian MarDock, *The First of Many: The Story of a Pioneering Chinese Family Who Lived in Texas for One Hundred Years* (Privately printed, 1998).

ted out of gratitude for their valuable services to his men. After numerous delays, officials sent about four hundred Chinese to the new military base being built in San Antonio. The Chinese helped clear the land and build Fort Travis, which became part of Fort Sam Houston. They also worked as cooks, laundrymen, and carpenters at other military posts in the city. After extensive litigation, these Chinese gained permanent residency in 1921 with most men remaining in San Antonio. Forever grateful to General Pershing, they honored him by giving their children names like Black Jack Wong and Pershing Yim.

With the arrival of "Pershing's Chinese," as they proudly considered themselves, San Antonio had the greatest concentration of Chinese in Texas. Many of the men opened shops and restaurants near the military bases. Using their designation as merchants, Chinese men in San Antonio brought in wives and young male relatives to work in their businesses. The community grew and prospered. In 1900 there had been only fifty-four Chinese in San Antonio, but by 1940 the number had grown to over five hundred. Seventy Chinese owned grocery stores, and nine had restaurants located throughout the city. Usually, Chinese homes were located near the family business with the entire family working for its success. In the 1920s and 1930s Chinese also ran laundries and stores in Houston, Galveston, Corsicana, Denison, Cleburne, El Paso, San Angelo, Tyler, and Amarillo.

Houston had a small Chinese population with only fifty in the city in 1930. Discrimination kept them out of the good jobs and the labor unions. Most Chinese families ran small groceries or restaurants and lived upstairs or behind the businesses. Chinese children attended public schools. Schools teaching Chinese language and culture did not exist until the 1970s. Some of the first Chinese professionals in Houston grew up in these settings. In the 1920s and 1930s the Chinese community in Houston grew with the arrival of Chinese who had been running small stores in rural Mississippi until many of their African American customers migrated north hoping for better jobs. When they arrived in Houston, the Chinese grocers

Herlinda Wong Chew, ca. 1916. Courtesy of the Wellington Chew family. Institute of Texan Cultures illustration

Herlinda Wong Chew

Herlinda Wong was born in Guadalajara, Mexico, the daughter of a Chinese man and an Aztec woman. She married Antonio Chew, the eldest son of a Chinese family who had come to Mexico. The couple opened a grocery store, La Garantia, in Ciudad Juárez. Mrs. Chew assisted her husband at the store and became acquainted with immigration officials. During the Mexican Revolution, she heard that a bloody battle would be fought in the city. By promising to return to Mexico, she and about two hundred of her friends were allowed to enter El Paso when the fighting began. Later she told of crossing the Rio Grande while dodging bullets and carrying her small children.

Following the revolution, Herlinda

Chinese men in a store in Valle, Mexico, December, 1916. Institute of Texan Cultures illustration no. 68-2965

Chinese and Mexican refugees leaving Mexico with the Pershing Expedition, January 28, 1917. Institute of Texan Cultures illustration no. 68-2966

continued to set up shops in the black areas of the city. Discrimination and prejudice against the Chinese continued in Houston, limiting their activities and job options.

The Chinese in San Antonio were more successful. They also had family-run shops but on a larger scale. Still, their experiences were difficult. Jim Eng grew up in San Antonio in the 1930s, living

The Joe Chew family outside their El Paso grocery store. Institute of Texan Cultures illustration no. 68-2980

Chew began to borrow and read books on immigration law. She learned that the Chinese could legally enter the United States if they were merchants. Making a claim to that effect, the Chews moved to El Paso in 1921. They opened the New China Grocery on River Street and later one on Stanton Street. Herlinda continued her study of immigration law, eventually being recognized as the local expert on immigration. In addition to acting as an interpreter, she used her knowledge to assist other Chinese in entering the United States and obtained visas for their visits to China. The Chews also escorted Chinese across the United States, guaranteeing their departure from San Francisco.

The Chews regularly took their eight children to China for their education. They would return for six months at

near the grocery store his family owned. The store sold to African Americans, Mexicans, and occasionally to whites. He described his parents' attitude toward the discriminatory practices they endured:

> Cause we were badly mistreated and the idea was to make some money and go back (to China) and retire and live. . . . [In addition to discriminatory immigration laws,] we're a minority, and lumped in with the Mexicans and not quite as bad as the blacks. We're discriminated against going certain places, and we'd never be able to join the San Antonio Country Club. And I don't think I ever wanted to, but there were places like swimming pools. Swimming pools, they were certainly off limits to us. . . . We know about that but our sole purpose in coming here was just to earn a living and saving and go back and be able to live. [My parents] don't really think of this being their country; they felt the resentment of the American community. They call us names and things like that.[4]

a time; the four boys would go with their father, then the four girls would go with Herlinda. While in China, Herlinda Chew observed the problems of Mexican women who had married Chinese men and gone to China with them. Locating seventy such women, she arranged to return them and their children to Mexico. In addition, Mrs. Chew organized independent shop owners of various nationalities in El Paso to create a wholesale buying unit to compete with chain stores. She was also appointed to work on minority issues as part of the National Recovery Act during the Depression.

Sources: Sarah John, "Herlinda Wong Chew: El Paso Trailblazer," *Password* 37, no. 1 (1992): 41–46; Chew sisters, oral history interview, El Paso, 1978, in the Southwest Collection, University of Texas at El Paso.

The Sam Leung grocery store located in San Antonio, ca. 1930. Institute of Texan Cultures illustration no. 76-472

Even with discrimination, some merchants did so well that in 1937 Texas representatives introduced a bill to deny the Chinese the right to own businesses because they were "not eligible for citizenship." The Texas Alien Land Law, passed ten years earlier, already denied Asians the right to own farmland, and the new legislation threatened the right of Chinese entering the state to own urban property as well. Chinese Texans effectively defended themselves at the legislative hearings in Austin by pointing out the factual errors and blatant self-interest of those promoting the bill. Mrs. T. H. Wu, the daughter of Chinese American citizens and the wife of a leading San Antonio Chinese merchant, would not be directly affected by the bill, but she protested, "I know I have the rights but I do not forget my blood. Every one can tell I am Chinese by my color."[5] The bill did not pass.

Board members of the Chinese school in San Antonio, ca. 1928. Institute of Texan Cultures illustration no. 68-2947

THE CULTURE OF THE EARLY CHINESE TEXANS

The San Antonio Chinese wanted more than economic success. They created kinship and business organizations to help other Chinese getting started or in need. They helped new arrivals find homes and jobs as well as investing in each other's businesses. After the Japanese attacked China in 1937, they collected money for refugees.

Girls in traditional dress stand in front of the El Paso Chinese School, ca. 1938. Institute of Texan Cultures illustration no. 68-2976

When civil war erupted between the Communist and Nationalist Chinese during World War II, many of the San Antonio Chinese supported Chiang Kai-shek, leader of the *Kuomintang*, the Nationalist Chinese. They created a local branch of the *Kuomintang* and celebrated the "Double 10," in honor of the beginning of the Republic of China on October 10, 1911.

Schools created by Chinese parents were perhaps the most valued of the organizations in San Antonio. After the day at public school, forty to fifty Chinese students attended a Chinese school from 4:30 to 7:30 six evenings a week. There they learned to read and write Chinese. Although the students spoke many Chinese dialects, all shared one written language based on word characters. The teacher read passages, and students repeated them aloud until they memorized them. The Chinese considered oral practice the best way to learn, and the class was full of students each reciting different passages at the same time. Students learned to draw Chinese word characters by tracing them in workbooks with a large brush and ink. The school also taught Chinese history, philosophy, and values such as honoring their elders. El Paso also had a similar school for Chinese children.

China was the home of several great religious traditions that blended and merged to form the foundation of Chinese life and culture. Confucian thought emphasized social harmony and order that was provided through good rulers and obedient followers. Within the hierarchy of families and nation, those with authority were respected. In contrast, Taoism proclaimed the paradoxical nature of life, the impossibility of sure knowledge, and the need to live with openness and humility. Buddhism, which originated in India, taught acceptance and loving kindness. Followers did not consider Buddha a god to be worshiped, but rather a man whose teachings and example were to be honored. Practicing one's beliefs in daily life was more important than formal gathering for worship. Folk religions often added gods and rituals to these major traditions.

Churches organized Christian missions for the Chinese in San Antonio as well as in El Paso and Houston. Initially, the missionaries in San Antonio provided Bible and English lessons to the Chinese who came with Pershing from Mexico. Later, the San Antonio mission became a formal church and joined the Southern Baptist Association. Sunday school and night classes were added for the

The Chinese Baptist Church in San Antonio following a rare snowstorm, January 30, 1949. Institute of Texan Cultures illustration no. 3694BB

Chinese children celebrate Halloween in San Antonio. Institute of Texan Cultures illustration no. 76-464

young men working in restaurants and grocery stores. One young Chinese woman visited mothers and, speaking to them in Chinese, told them about Christianity while the children learned about Easter egg hunts, Halloween, and Santa Claus.

The absence of temples, monks, and families hampered other kinds of religious activity among the Chinese who first worked in Texas. Yet the Chinese regularly observed the traditional Lunar New Year. In Robertson County 150 Chinese paraded in the streets on their first New Year's celebration. In the coming years, the Chinese celebrated various occasions all along the railroads they were building in West Texas. Their non-Chinese neighbors watched the festivals with curiosity and frequently commented on the noise, not understanding that the purpose of the firecrackers was to scare off evil in the coming year.

A reporter in a 1904 El Paso newspaper presented his stereotypical, but popular view of the Chinese New Year celebration:

> Tomorrow evening the Chinese inhabitants of the Pass City . . . will inaugurate their annual new year celebration, a festival that lasts for two weeks, and it will therefore be several days before they get down to business in proper style and resume their occupations of washing shirts, selling hash, and hitting the consoling pipe of the Orient [opium]. For two weeks the Celestials [people from China, the Celestial city or nation] of El Paso will be all agog over their festivals. New Year is a great event with the heathen Chinese. The followers of Confucius are loyal in their adherence to the customs of the flowery kingdom and no length of residence among the "Melican" [Mexican] people can wean from them the celebration of the anniversary.
>
> It is during the New Year season that the Celestial truly shines. For the period he comes out of his shell of stoicism and indifference in which the Christian always finds him and is a truly lovable being.[6]

Chinese held the Dragon Boat Festival in early summer on the "Double 5," or the fifth day of the fifth month. This event commemorated a Chinese folk hero who drowned himself when his advice was not heeded and he was dismissed from service to the ruler. According to the story, villagers in boats raced to find him and tossed sweet, sticky rice balls into the river for him. Celebrating these events, Chinese held river races in long, narrow boats decorated with dragon heads and tails. The boats contained crews of up to twenty paddling to the beat of an onboard drummer. The dragon represented strength and goodness. They ate fist-sized rice balls wrapped in lotus leaves and filled with salted pork, nuts, and egg yolks. As with every Chinese

Chinese Lunar New Year

For Chinese the New Year begins with the first new moon of the year, which usually occurs in late January or early February. Traditionally, preparation takes place before the New Year begins. Homes and shops are cleaned and food cooked in advance because knives and brooms cannot be used on the first day of the year for fear of "cutting" or "sweeping" away good luck. Scrolls and banners are hung, often red ones. All financial debts must be paid before the old year ends, and all quarrels are to be settled. Everyone who can afford to do so gets new clothes or at least new shoes for the New Year.

As the New Year approaches, families offer the paper image of the Kitchen God, Tsao Chur, sweet foods and

Chinese dragon-head mask used in New Year celebrations. Institute of Texan Cultures illustration no. 68-2983

celebration, there were lots of firecrackers to scare off evil spirits and sometimes there were shadow puppet shows of ancient legends. Both Austin and Houston hold Dragon Boat Festivals in the spring of each year.

In the fall, the Chinese held a Moon Festival. People lay on the ground and watched the moon. They offered food and incense to the Moon Lady, who they hoped would grant special secret wishes at this time. Celebrants served moon cakes, the roundness of which suggested harmony and unity. Often the cakes were stamped with designs and had egg yolks at the center or sweet fillings of bean paste or coconut.

Red Egg Festivals were held for month-old babies. The infant's head was shaved and rubbed with a red egg for good luck. A cap with lucky charms was then placed on the baby's head. Babies also received gifts of tiger slippers, because tigers' sharp eyes were believed to keep the baby from slipping when learning to walk. Guests received red-dyed eggs and often a meal of pigs' feet and chicken cooked in whiskey. Another custom was for parents to set out various objects, and the objects grabbed by the baby were believed to determine the baby's future.

Chinese Texans followed traditional Chinese burial customs as much as possible. In El Paso, caretakers at Concordia Cemetery designated a special section for Chinese burials. On the way to the cemetery, the Chinese people held parades and were often accompanied by hired bands. Once a fifty-foot paper dragon led the funeral procession down the streets with the men who wore it guiding its movements. The guests said traditional prayers and placed food and flowers on the grave for the departed spirit's journey. Paper representations of earthly possessions were burned for use by the dead in the afterlife. The family distributed candy and money, often wrapped in "lucky" red paper, to remind everyone that despite death, life was sweet.

China is known as the source of the martial arts and its influence was felt in both Japan and Korea. Martial arts, or unarmed combat, originated to protect peaceful monks. Over the centuries, different techniques for unarmed fighting emerged. The Chinese martial art of kung fu literally means hard work and perfection. Some participants concentrated on the use of circular arm and hand movements while others emphasized the use of high, powerful kicks.

In Texas the Chinese ate their traditional foods and used chopsticks. Sticky rice served as the basis of most meals with meat and vegetables added whenever possible. Many Chinese women cultivated small gardens so they could have their traditional vegetables such as the distinctive Chinese celery and cabbage. Preserved eggs that were soaked in salt water for forty days before being cooked and eaten were a rare delicacy for the Chinese.

The Chinese had become a permanent part of Texas before World War II, despite the limitations on their immigration. They continued traditional practices though many of them began accepting Christianity. They were not, however, fully integrated into the life of Texas.

smear his mouth with honey so that he will say good things about them. Then they burn the image so that the smoke will carry him to the heavens. According to legend Tsao Chur visits the heavens every year and reports to the Jade Sunperson on each family member's good and bad behaviors.

New Year's Eve is a time for family feasting and honoring the families' ancestors. Families gather for a shared meal. Food is also placed on shrines so that ancestors may join the family feast. Firecrackers, invented in China, are exploded to frighten the evil spirits.

On New Year's Day, the feasting and honoring of ancestors continues along with more firecrackers. Food symbolizing wishes for the future is served. People wear their new clothes and shoes and think only kind and good thoughts in order to receive kindness and good luck throughout the year. The day is considered everyone's birthday with all a year older. The Chinese count age by the Lunar New Year, rather than the actual date of birth.

Family and friends visit each other, giving gifts of fruit and small amounts of money that are always presented in even denominations to ward off bad luck. Oranges representing gold or wealth are prized gifts. Nien-gao, *a rice pudding made with sticky rice, indicates family unity and hopes for the coming year. Long grain rice is given to encourage longevity, and dried oysters represent good undertakings and good business. Rice cakes, candied fruits, and vegetables are also served.*

Children receive lucky red envelopes with

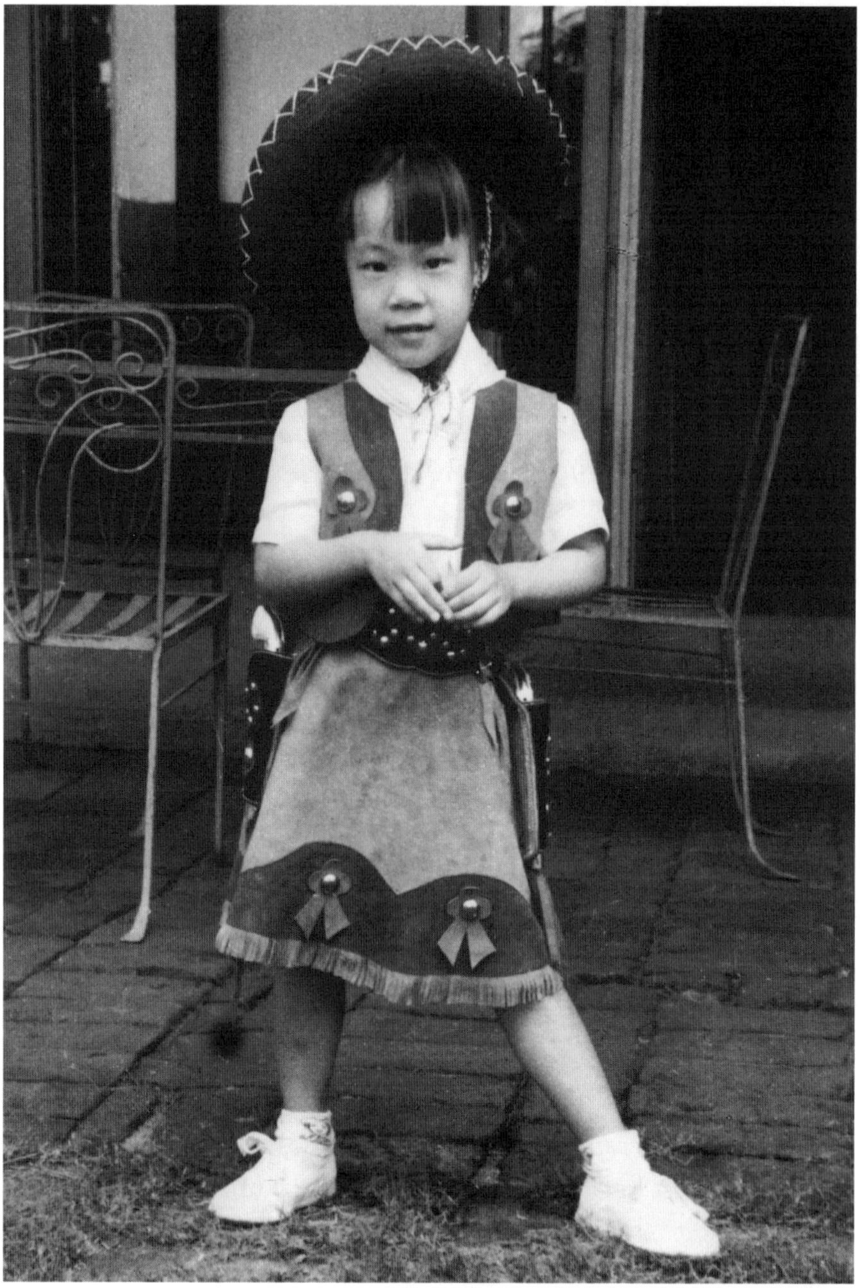

San Antonio Chinese children play "dress up" cowboys and cowgirls. Institute of Texan Cultures illustration nos. 76-449 and 76-445

an even number of bills or coins stuffed inside. Odd numbers are considered bad luck. Dancers parade in the streets, and a paper dragon wiggles along on the backs of several men.

Celebrating goes on for two weeks and concludes with the Lantern Festival, held at the first full moon of the year. Lanterns of all kinds are paraded through the streets along with a massive paper dragon, thought to bring strength and goodness to the celebrants.

Source: Carol Stepanchuk, *Red Eggs and Dragon Boats: Celebrating Chinese Festivals* (Berkeley, Calif.: Pacific View Press, 1994).

CHINESE TEXANS AFTER WORLD WAR II

Chinese immigrants were the first group of people to be excluded from immigration to the United States, and it was not until 1943 that Congress formally lifted the ban on their entry. During World War II, China allied with the United States against their traditional enemy, Japan. Texas Chinese joined the military and worked in defense plants. To show appreciation for the Chinese contribution to the war effort, national legislators passed laws that granted the Chinese permission to start the process of becoming citizens. New laws also benefited men from the U.S. military who had brought home war brides from China. Some Chinese American men who fought in the Pacific were able to bring the wives they had married decades earlier to the United States under the provisions of these laws. The number of Chinese women in Texas finally began to grow.

As World War II neared an end, civil war broke out in China between the *Kuomintang*, or Nationalists, and Chinese Communist forces. Some Chinese left their homeland and entered the United

Chinese Texans collected for the Chinese Relief Fund during the Japanese invasion of their homeland. Institute of Texan Cultures illustration no. 76-486

Meeting of the southern branch of the San Antonio Kuomintang, a Chinese Nationalist organization that formed during the civil war with the Communist Chinese. Institute of Texan Cultures illustration no. 76-483

States as refugees. In 1949 the Chinese Communists gained control of mainland China. Nationalist Chinese settled on the island of Formosa, now known as Taiwan. Many Chinese Texans supported the *Kuomintang* in the 1940s.

In the 1970s many Chinese who lived in Vietnam, Cambodia, and Laos came to the United States as refugees. Since then, other Chinese have left mainland China, which is controlled by the Communist Chinese. Whatever side they take in regard to their homeland, Chinese Texans have been loyal to the United States, and many have stayed permanently and become U.S. citizens.

Although the early Chinese in Texas were primarily laborers from southern China who spoke Cantonese, the newest arrivals represent groups from various regions of China with many now speaking Mandarin. They come as professionals, doctors, and scientists or as students. Chinese men and women now work in space and biomedical research, electronics and aerospace manufacture, and petroleum and petrochemical production, especially in Houston,

Gene Lee and his son Sam in their Houston print shop where they published the Southwest Chinese Journal. Institute of Texan Cultures illustration no. 76-461

which now has the largest Chinese population in the state. Chinese doctors are also establishing medical practices in smaller cities like Midland and Lubbock. Some new Chinese immigrants work as skilled laborers and technicians or open shops and restaurants as they did in the past.

The entry of large numbers of Chinese has led to the creation of ethnic communities and institutions in major Texas cities with clusters of new Chinese families and businesses. Yet none of the strict isolation that once characterized ethnic neighborhoods exists. Many

Chinese have substantial incomes, especially if a man and wife are both employed professionals. Employment alongside white professionals is common. The education of their children, a traditional Chinese value, is important in their choice of homes. The children of Chinese Texans are often more strictly disciplined than their non-Asian peers. A young Chinese Texan woman explains her parents' discipline:

> I admit there is not as much freedom in my house as in typical American households, but I am used to it and have grown to cherish it as a part of my culture. I have grown to be 19, and I am very happy. This should prove that my parents must have done something right.
>
> I hated discipline as much as the next kid on the block, but I now recognize this discipline as part of my culture, a culture that has given me inner strength which pushes me to be a hard worker and a better person. . . . Now that I am in college, I no longer have a curfew. This would be unheard of in China, Taiwan or Hong Kong today. It says my parents trust me enough to let me make my own decisions.[7]

A major concentration of Chinese businesses, restaurants, and organizations in southwest Houston has created a new Chinatown. Investment from Chinese Texan professionals has helped fund the businesses there. Street signs are in Chinese characters, a symbol of the rising importance of the Chinese Texans in the city. An older Chinatown, now a historic district, also exists near downtown Houston and is frequented by the descendants of earlier Chinese Texans.

Schools that teach the Chinese language and customs to the younger generation are present in several Texas cities, and cultural centers provide films and secular events. By 2000 Houston's Chinese population had risen to 48,294, and there were over thirty Chinese Protestant churches, four Buddhist temples, and one temple to traditional Chinese deities. Many of the newer churches are evangelical and reject traditional practices that they see as contradicting Christianity. Usually newcomers worship separately from the pre–World War II immigrants and their descendants. Nonetheless, Chinese

Texans find ways to retain their cultural identity while adapting to their new lives by being part of Chinese Christian churches.

Other Chinese continue to practice Buddhism. In China, Buddhism focuses primarily on the *sanga,* or community of monks who perform chants and meditations. Chinese Buddhists in Texas, however, are moving toward more involvement of laypeople and more emphasis on everyday life. Non-Chinese sometimes join their worship, attracted to the meditation and serenity fostered by Buddhism.

Buddhist temples contain a large statue of Buddha. Incense, bells, and drums are used in worship. Worshipers traditionally bow before the Buddha and join the monks who lead the service in chanting and meditation. In a room nearby are floor cushions and ancestral tablets where offerings are placed. One Buddhist tradition followed for many years in Houston was the *fang sheng* in which people purchased fresh crabs from a local seafood market and took them to a beach in Galveston where they were released. After returning the crabs to the sea, they enjoyed a picnic. The *fang sheng* was an ancient ritual based on the liberation of living things.

Chinese in other Texas towns also continued secular celebrations that were at least as old as China's religions. The Lunar New Year was still the most important festival. Sometimes Chinese joined with Vietnamese, Koreans, and other Asians for a larger celebration with foods, dances, and parades. Sometimes the Chinese Buddhist temples gave each person attending a lucky red envelope containing a dollar bill. Folk dances, songs, martial arts, and Chinese children's games were all part of the festivities, which lead to the Lantern Festival, two weeks later. Chinese also celebrated the Dragon Boat Festival, Moon Festival, and the Red Egg Ceremony.

After the loosening of immigration restrictions in 1965, a large wave of Chinese immigrants entered Texas. They are now the third largest Asian group in the state with 112,950 people reporting at least one Chinese parent in the 2000 census. As they continue to celebrate their own institutions and customs, they add a culturally rich heritage to the state of Texas.

CHAPTER 2
Japanese Texans

LIKE THE CHINESE, Japanese settlers began coming to Texas at a time when massive change was occurring in their homeland. In 1858 Admiral Matthew Perry's arrival had forced Japanese leaders to accept a trade treaty with the United States that ended two centuries of Japan's isolation from the rest of the world. The existing Japanese government fell, and the new leadership favored modernization and industrialization. By the early 1900s Japan had begun a drive to become an industrial power. As change swept the country, economic hardship caused many Japanese to seek new ways to earn a living. Pamphlets and articles about the opportunities in the United States circulated throughout Japan.

Traditionally, young Japanese men left their homes to work elsewhere in Japan and contribute to the family income. By the 1890s they were also going to Hawaii, California, and other points along the Pacific Coast to labor on sugar plantations, on railroads, and in fisheries. They toiled for farmers, raising a variety of crops to feed the growing American cities. As "schoolboys" learning English, they worked in the homes and gardens of the wealthy. Like the Chinese and European immigrants along the East Coast, they provided the labor necessary for the growth of the American nation. Eventually these young men hoped to earn enough money to return to Japan. Other Japanese men migrated to Mexico to work on the railroads or in the mines, including the coal mines at Muzquiz, Mexico. Some men entered the United States from the south and were among the first Japanese to settle in Texas. By 1900 a handful of Japanese were

The Japanese in Houston gathered at Tom Brown Okasaki's "Japanese Cafe" for celebrations. Both the Japanese and U.S. flags hang from the ceiling. Institute of Texan Cultures illustration nos. 95-603 and 95-602

living in El Paso, Dallas, and Houston where they worked primarily as laborers.

In Houston some early Japanese arrivals in Texas opened restaurants, as they continued to do throughout the century. Starting a small café required little cash and little knowledge of English. These restaurants usually served inexpensive American-style meals and were popular with working-class people. A major figure in the emergence of the Houston Japanese community was restaurant owner Tsunekichi Okasaki, known as Tom Brown. He opened his "Japanese Restaurant" in downtown Houston in the 1890s, selling meals for ten to twenty-five cents. Many Japanese Texans worked for him when they first arrived in Houston. Gradually, he branched out, trying rice farming in 1907 and starting the Japan Art and Tea Company in 1911. He also opened two more restaurants, including one that served Japanese food.

In 1903 educated and prosperous Japanese men began purchasing land and moving to Texas. They differed sharply from the laborers who dreamed of returning to Japan. Most were second and third sons of prominent *samurai* families who had held powerful social and military roles before the reorganization of Japanese society. These Japanese immigrants hoped to establish colonies near Houston to grow rice. Arriving with their wives, children, and sometimes their parents, they came planning to create large, permanent communities. With money to invest and the ability to obtain additional loans, they had the resources to undertake such ventures. As colonists, they encouraged young single Japanese men, often from their home regions in Japan, to come and work for them in the rice fields. Starting as laborers, these men dreamed that they could eventually lease land and become landowners themselves.

A few unsuccessful attempts had been made to grow rice along the Gulf Coast before the Japanese Consul General Sadatsuchi Uchida visited Houston in 1902. City leaders assured him of their interest in establishing rice colonies owned and run by Japanese. Uchida published information in Japan about the possibilities of growing rice in Texas and talked about the opportunities with his friends.

Seito Saibara
Seito Saibara was born in southern Japan in 1861. At the Risshisha English School, he studied European political theorists and got involved in politics. Seito continued his education and obtained a law degree from the Shigematsu Law School. In 1899 he was asked to be president of Doshisha University, a Christian college. While college president, he continued to serve in the Japanese parliament. In 1902 he came to the United States, initially to study theology. After contact with a Japanese consul who had visited Texas, he decided to stay in the United States and start a rice plantation. Arriving in Houston in 1903, he bought land on the railroad near Webster. The next year more Japanese arrived, including Saibara's wife. Special high quality rice seed was imported from

Seito Saibara was the first Japanese whom Uchida convinced to start a rice plantation. When Saibara arrived in Houston in 1903, he met bank presidents, newspaper editors, and the "colonization agent" for the Southern Pacific Railroad, which had land to sell. Following Uchida's advice, Saibara purchased land on the railroad near Webster, just south of Houston. Investors from both Houston and Japan loaned him money for his venture. His family and people from his home area in Japan soon joined the new colony. To entice settlers to his colony he promised wages to those who were unable to purchase land themselves. He paid an additional bonus for wives who came with their husbands. Like other Japanese colonizers to follow him, Saibara viewed economic enterprise as communal, to be engaged in as a group, not as an individual effort.

The Saibara rice plantation quickly became successful and famous. Distinguished Japanese visited the colony, wrote about it, and encouraged others to follow Saibara's example. The Louisiana Purchase Exhibition, held in St. Louis, Missouri, in 1904, included a display of Texas rice. Japanese business leaders and members of the Japanese Parliament made a trip to Saibara's colony after they had visited the exhibition. Soon other Japanese colonies were created near Houston. Rihei Onishi, an international journalist, and his cousin, Toraichi, established a large, successful rice colony near Saibara's. Sen Katayama, a noted Japanese socialist, also tried to start a rice colony, but his venture failed.

The risk of crop failure was great. Droughts and hurricanes frequently destroyed rice crops. Prices for rice were initially high, but after World War I, they fell. Rice farmers responded by diversifying their crops, raising cotton and vegetables, or turning to the nursery business.

Raising rice involved lots of hard work. Land had to be cleared and levees built to hold the water needed to grow the rice. The men planted rice by pulling huge drums across the fields to distribute the seed. The fields were then flooded with six to eight inches of water provided by networks of irrigation ditches and paddle wheels. When the rice was mature, workers drained the fields. After the fields had

Seito Saibara. Institute of Texan Cultures illustration no. 95-600

Japan, and soon the Japanese were raising two to three times more rice per acre than other Texas rice farmers. Saibara had established the first successful rice farm in Texas.

As soon as he reached Texas, Saibara filed to become a citizen of the United States. Citizenship was denied him, however, because of the 1790 naturalization law that allowed only whites to become citizens. Saibara wanted to challenge this law, but Japanese officials convinced him not to do so. In 1922 the law forbidding citizenship to Asians was upheld. Disillusioned with the verdict and with the national law prohibiting Japanese entry into the United States, Saibara and his wife moved to Brazil. His son continued to run the rice farm in Texas. In 1937, while in his seventies, he was allowed to return to

Texas to be with his family only because of his friendship with a high-ranking official in Washington.

Sources: Kiyoko Tanabe, "The Japanese Immigrant in the Houston–Harris County Area," (master's thesis, Rice University, 1956), pp. 8–27; Thomas Wall, *Japanese Texans* (San Antonio: Institute of Texan Cultures, 1987), pp. 42–54, 76–

Japanese men at work in rice fields at Webster, Texas, in 1905. Saibara stands third from the right. Institute of Texan Cultures illustration no. 86-308

dried, heavy horse-drawn machinery cut the rice stalks and bound them into shocks. Steam winnows were sometimes used to separate the rice kernel from the chaff. American workers initially drove the threshers accompanied by Japanese, who learned how to run the machines. Mexican, Cajun, and African workers labored alongside the Japanese during harvest.

In 1907 and 1908 the governments of the United States and Japan entered a "Gentlemen's Agreement" to limit Japanese immigration to the United States. Laborers were forbidden to come, although merchants and students could continue to enter. "Settled agriculturists," such as the Houston rice growers, could return to Japan for visits and then reenter the United States—a privilege denied to many others. Under the new agreement, Japanese women were allowed into the United States only if their husbands already lived there.

The majority of Japanese Texans were single young men who wanted to marry, but few unmarried Japanese women had immigrated. Some men returned to Japan to marry and bring their wives back to Texas. Some married Mexican women. Others chose to marry "picture brides." With the new immigration restrictions, arranged marriages took on increased significance. Single Japanese men asked those in their home villages to arrange a possible marriage for them.

The potential bride and groom then exchanged pictures by mail and, using a male stand-in as the temporary groom, were married in Japan. The newly married bride then sailed to the United States to meet her husband and start her new life.

Immigration officials at Angel Island, the Pacific Coast entry point for Asians, frequently did not believe that the Japanese marriages had taken place. They often caused delays and forced the new wives to return to Japan. One group of Texas rice growers tried to

Japanese workers at the flume that carried water between the well house and the irrigation canal on a rice farm at El Campo, Texas. Institute of Texan Cultures illustration no. 86-238

bring a group of picture brides for their workers, but the brides were refused entry at Angel Island. The resourceful women sailed to Mexico, entered the United States through Eagle Pass, and eventually joined their new husbands.

With the marriages and arrival of the women, more Japanese started families. Traditionally, Japanese held children in high regard and had large families. The children attended public schools near their homes and quickly learned to read and speak English. At home their mothers told the children Japanese folk tales, taught them the Japanese language, and carried out familiar cultural rituals. Houston had no formal Japanese school, but two Japanese women taught small groups of children about their traditions.

When the first Japanese arrived in the Houston area, they immediately tried to become U.S. citizens. They were forbidden to do so because of the naturalization law of 1790 that only allowed citizenship for "whites."[1] The children of immigrants, however, were U.S. citizens because they were born in this country. The generation of Japanese who had immigrated were declared aliens and known as Issei, and the second generation, who were born citizens, Nisei. Having children who were U.S. citizens increased the commitment that the Issei felt toward the United States.

In 1907 and 1908 Kichimatsu Kishi founded one of the more successful early Japanese colonies in Texas. The son of a large landowner, Kishi had studied business at a prestigious Japanese college and fought in the Russian-Japanese War. Seeking to become a landowner himself, he came to the United States and purchased land suitable for rice farming along the Southern Pacific Railroad at Terry, located between Beaumont and Orange. He brought his large family and other Japanese to Terry where hard work brought them some success. Later, picture brides joined the single men who had earned enough money to build their own homes.

In the 1920s a researcher who visited the Kishi colony made the following observations:

Rice harvest for the Onishi family near Webster, Texas, in 1908. Institute of Texan Cultures illustration no. 86-273

Mr. Kishi is Americanized and adheres to the Christian religion. He takes an active part in religious work in the colony; is a member of the Orange County Rotary Club; and is interested in all the progressive problems that confront Orange County. Mr. Kishi's home in this colony is a two-story frame building, modestly and comfortably furnished with American-made furniture.

Mr. Kishi engages the services of a railroad freight agent during the harvest seasons. He employs a marketing expert, who goes north and west to get the best prices; an accountant, who keeps careful account of every foot of ground under cultivation, and to the pound and cent knows what each acre of land is doing; a private secretary, and a general manager. American-made machinery and practically the same methods of farming that Americans use are used in this colony.

Torata Akagi, son of Ju and Fukutaro Akagi, is pictured here in western dress. He stayed in Japan with his cousins before joining his parents at a farm north of Houston. Institute of Texan Cultures illustration no. 78-39

> The families in the colony are large, having from four to eight children in each. These children, however, are well trained by their parents, who spend a great deal of their time teaching them the difference between right and wrong. The children are intelligent and learn very rapidly. They dress like Americans, except that the girls' dresses are longer than those worn by American girls. Some of the Japanese girls wear long hair. As a rule, the children are neat in appearance.
>
> The impression one receives of this colony is that it is well organized, contented, and prosperous, and is thoroughly American in its practices and ideals.[2]

However, even the well-financed and well-managed Kishi colony had problems. When contractors deepened the Sabine River Channel, salt water flowed into the colony's irrigated fields, destroying the rice. Not able to continue growing rice, Kishi and his workers had to diversify their crops and began growing a variety of vegetables that did not need extensive irrigation. Cabbage became a particularly profitable crop, yielding one hundred carloads a year by the late 1920s. The colony also grew cotton, corn, sweet potatoes,

Fuji and Kichimatsu Kishi pose with their children, relatives, and servant. Institute of Texan Cultures illustration no. 68-3002

Wagons filled with rice arrive in Bay City, Texas, from nearby Japanese colonies, ca. 1901. Institute of Texan Cultures illustration no. 86-240

cauliflower, and lettuce. As he prospered, Kishi expanded his land holdings and equipment. The colony owned thirty-five teams of horses and mules as well as tractors, threshers, and other machinery.

Rice prices fell after World War I, forcing more and more Japanese to stop growing rice and to start growing vegetables. With only tiny plots of land available in Japan, the men were experienced in the "intensive farming" that allowed them to grow large quantities of produce in a small area. Residents of Houston and other Gulf towns were eager to buy the fresh produce, which the Japanese men trucked into nearby towns. Mitsutaro Kobayashi had worked in shipyards and orchards before meeting Saibara and coming to Texas. After serving as an engineer for rice farmers, he began his own farm and successfully shipped vegetables to several states.

Fukutaro Akagi initially worked on the sugar plantations in Hawaii and then on railroads and in mines throughout the western United States. He left his wife, Ju, and son, Torata, in Japan for twelve years before Ju joined him in a mining camp. In the camp she contributed to the family income by taking in laundry. When their son was about fifteen years old, he also joined them, and the couple began a successful farming venture near Houston.

The rich farmland of the Rio Grande Valley also attracted Japanese farmers from Houston. Railroads and irrigation were being introduced, making farming in the region profitable after 1900. Slowly, Japanese Texans moved to the area and began clearing the land, digging irrigation ditches, and growing vegetables. Heishiro Miyamoto, who came to the Mission area in 1908, was among the first to arrive. By 1920 a dozen Japanese families had farms near Mission and San Benito. Several families established a cooperative farm near Brownsville. They grew cotton and sugarcane as well as vegetables. Japanese truckers transported their produce to locations outside the Valley.

Beginning in 1903, El Paso civic leaders encouraged Japanese farmers to come to their city. The El Paso Chamber of Commerce hoped to make El Paso the only silk-producing center in the United States. The Chamber arranged for the U.S. Department of Agriculture to provide silkworm eggs to the Japanese farmers and donate the mulberry trees needed to feed the silkworms. The silk project experiment failed, but the Japanese along the Rio Grande to the

Saburo Arai, on the right, and workers at his "Japanese Nurseries" in Houston. Institute of Texan Cultures illustration no. 86-368

Saburo Arai

Saburo Arai was born the third son of a samurai *family in Niigata Prefecture in Japan. Because he had no hope of inheriting from his father, he was adopted by a wholesaler. Eventually, he ran away to Tokyo and studied English in a Catholic school before sailing to the United States in 1884 at the age of eighteen. In California he worked as a "school boy," doing manual labor for room and board while completing high school. He also studied horticulture, Latin, Greek, and law and converted to Christianity.*

Arai created an exhibit for the 1904 World's Fair. It consisted of a miniature Japanese village with tiny plants and people performing traditional music, dance, and wrestling. After a brief trip to Japan, he tried

Wedding portrait of Uichi and Takako Shimotsu, who were among the first Japanese farmers to settle near McAllen, Texas, in the Rio Grande Valley. Prior to immigrating, they both graduated from college and married in 1916. Institute of Texan Cultures illustration no. 85-935

north and the east became successful farmers, growing vegetables and raising poultry.

Daito Ishiroku came to the United States where he worked first as a miner and cook. He married a woman from his village back home, and the couple purchased farmland southeast of El Paso in the Rio Grande floodplain. Imai Takeo originally migrated to Mexico where jobs were available in the mines and railroads. When he came to El Paso, he worked as a shoe repairman and restaurant owner before obtaining a farm where he raised chicken, rabbits, and vegetables, which he sold at Fort Bliss.

Immigration officers tried to stop the Japanese from crossing into El Paso from Mexico. Claiming that "thousands" of Asians and Middle Easterners were crossing the border, the immigration authorities urged that all laws and regulations be enforced. When Japan agreed to withhold passports from laborers intending to migrate to the United States in the "Gentlemen's Agreement" of 1907 and 1908, the smuggling of Japanese, like the smuggling of Chinese, became a big business along the border. Railroad conductors, immigration officials, and ordinary citizens all became involved in smuggling rings. Japanese who were caught often claimed to be "just passing through" on their way to Canada, but the immigration officials forced many to return to Japan. In 1907 fifty-five Japanese from Eagle Pass, twenty-nine from Laredo, eight from San Antonio, and seven from El Paso were sent to San Francisco for deportation.

During the Mexican Revolution when the fighting neared the border city of Juárez, the Immigration Service suspended the rules for both Japanese and Chinese, which allowed them to enter El Paso. Some Japanese remained in El Paso to open grocery stores and other businesses.

JAPANESE TEXAN COMMUNITIES, 1920–40

By 1920 Japanese communities existed in El Paso and the Rio Grande Valley as well as in Houston. Most Japanese were farmers, but some

growing rice near El Campo. Then in 1910 he bought a nursery in Alvin where he introduced mandarin orange trees. When a bad freeze killed the trees, he sold the mineral rights to his land to Humble Oil Company to save his nursery. Arai went on to become an outstanding nurseryman in Houston. He designed major landscape projects for the city of Houston and Humble Oil. At its peak, his nursery employed about one hundred people, some of them Japanese immigrants seeking to learn the nursery business.

Saburo's wife, Kyoko, cooked and fed the seventy to one hundred men who worked at the nursery and created a Bible study group for Japanese women, which lasted over a decade. A Japanese contractor from California designed the Arais' home in Houston in a traditional Japanese style. The paper sliding doors, alcoves, and stair-step bookcases helped make the home comfortable to Japanese visitors.

When the Texas legislature tried to end the ownership of land by Japanese, Arai led the opposition. He organized Japanese Texans to lobby against the bill and showed that claims about escalating land ownership by Japanese were false.

After the Japanese bombing of Pearl Harbor, Aria's nursery closed for a month. When the nursery reopened, it had a new name. As Kyoko Arai said: "We decided to erase 'Japanese' in order not to antagonize the people. We took off signs, threw out stationery, and rubbed the signs off the trucks."

Sources: Tanabe, "Japanese Immigrant," pp. 54–57; Wall, *Japanese Texans*, pp. 121–27, 154–55.

had small businesses and lived in other Texas cities. Warm relationships often existed between individual Japanese Texans and their neighbors, but hostility toward the Japanese as a group began to build.

Initially, the Japanese had been welcomed to Texas as rice farmers, but as hostility toward them developed along the Pacific Coast, some Texans also began to resent their presence. California, where jealousy and hatred were the worst, passed a law in 1920 forbidding Japanese immigrants to own land. After the passage of the California Land Law, the Japanese began to migrate from the West Coast to Texas, either joining others near Houston, taking up farming in the Rio Grande Valley, or settling near El Paso.

Some Texans in El Paso and the Valley were frightened by this "invasion" of Japanese into the state. They brought in national speakers to convince Texans of the supposed danger of this foreign element in their midst. In Harlingen a committee of citizens told Japanese families who had arrived to leave.

> FAMILY TOLD TO MOVE ON
>
> Harlingen, Tex., Jan. 6—Two families of Japanese who arrived in Harlingen Wednesday from the West intending to settle on farming lands were met at the railroad station and informed by a committee of citizens that their presence was undesirable in Harlingen and told that they could remain over night, but were "expected to leave" Thursday.[3]

The American Legion pressured the Texas legislature to pass a law forbidding the Japanese from owning land. The Texas legislature passed the Alien Land Law in 1921, but Japanese Texans had enough political influence to weaken it. The law stated that new arrivals to Texas could not purchase land, but Japanese who already owned land could keep it. Without the hope of owning land, few Japanese desired to settle in the state.

Saburo Arai, a nurseryman from Houston, led the fight against the land law prohibiting Japanese from owning property. When it was passed, he had this to say: "It appears to us that for so great a nation as this not to allow an industrious and law abiding people, already admitted into her domain the right of citizenship; and now to attempt confiscation of the privilege of owning land; for her labor unions to refuse admittance into their organizations; in fact, to shut off from them every avenue of becoming good and loyal citizens is a serious national crime, regrettably inconsistent with the spirit on which this nation was founded."[4]

Meanwhile, people throughout the United States exerted pressure on government representatives to limit all immigration. The immigration bill passed by Congress in 1924 established quotas for the number of European immigrants admitted from each country. It also declared that no Asians could enter the United States or become citizens. With few exceptions, all Asian immigration stopped.

The exclusion of further immigration from Japan compounded the problems faced by the Texas Japanese who had been here for several decades. Some Japanese from Texas as well as from other states returned to Japan. However, Japanese Texans continued to have children so the number of Japanese in the state remained stable.

Where families lived near each other, Japanese came together around events and newly created organizations. As the Nisei, or second generation of Japanese Texans, became teenagers, organizations were created for them in Houston and in the Rio Grande Valley. The "Lone Star" and the "Rio Grande Club" hosted dances and other events for the young Japanese Texans.

The Japanese community in and near El Paso thrived in the years before World War II. Although not allowed to purchase land, farmers leased property and prospered by selling vegetables and poultry. Small businesses were easy to establish and did well. Some of the Issei men in El Paso married Mexican women. They lived in the Mexican parts of town, became Roman Catholics, took Mexican first names and nicknames, and had stores that sold goods to Mexican customers. Their children, isolated from the other Japanese, were more likely to think of themselves as Mexican than Japanese.

Dr. Sadakazu Furugochi

Sadakazu Furugochi was born in Japan and immigrated to California where he practiced medicine and married. When California passed laws in 1920 to prohibit Japanese from owning land, he and his wife moved to El Paso. Dr. Furugochi provided medical assistance to the city's small Japanese community and to poor Mexicans. He delivered babies for free, and when patients could not pay his two-dollar fee, he treated them anyway.

Dr. Furugochi became a leader in the Japanese community. He retained contacts with the Japanese government and arranged for visits to El Paso by a Japanese ambassador, the first Japanese pilot to fly across the Pacific, and other leading Japanese. Visitors met Anglo leaders like the mayor

Young Nisei play "Flying Dutchman" at a gathering in San Benito, Texas, ca. 1940. Institute of Texan Cultures illustration no. 79-325

Japanese Texans at League City, Texas, enjoy an Easter picnic in 1936. Institute of Texan Cultures illustration no. 78-49

El Paso Japanese established a Japanese language school for the Nisei. The El Paso Nippon Gakuen was modeled after similar schools on the West Coast. Children learned the language and customs of their parents' homeland after having spent the day in public schools. The outspoken, individualistic behavior that they learned from teachers and other children in the public schools sharply contradicted the quiet, obedient demeanor demanded at the Japanese school.

In El Paso the Japanese created the Japanese American Association as early as 1915. It lasted until World War II, providing a social gathering place for men to converse in Japanese and discuss events. Members regularly celebrated traditional Japanese holidays, observing the emperor's birthday at San Juan Hall. In 1934 they marked the birth of the crown prince with a special celebration.

Hostility toward the Japanese appeared in El Paso during the 1930s, however. When Japan invaded China in 1937, the Chinese in El Paso put up signs asking customers to boycott Japanese stores and products. Although Japanese Texans felt that they had assimilated to their new country, they continued to be perceived as different by those around them. Pressure on the Japanese Texans got worse before it got better.

THE CULTURE OF THE JAPANESE TEXANS

Buddhism had originated in sixth-century India, and monks later brought it to Japan where it flourished. All Buddhists followed a set of guidelines called the Five Precepts:

> Do not harm or kill things.
> Do not take things unless they are freely given.
> Lead a decent life.
> Do not speak unkindly or tell lies.
> Do not take drugs or drink alcohol.

and attended receptions in their honor at Fort Bliss. Furugochi also spoke on Japan at the college and helped found the Japanese school, El Paso Nippon Gakuen.

After the bombing of Pearl Harbor, however, Dr. Furugochi lost the good will of his neighbors in El Paso. The F.B.I. arrested Japanese men in the city. Furugochi had an interest in radios, and on the day of the bombing, the F.B.I. located him in the Franklin Mountains repairing radio antennae and assumed he was a spy. He was sent to an internment camp in Santa Fe. When Japanese began to be released in 1943, Dr. Furugochi remained at the camp giving medical assistance. He died in 1973 after a lifetime of service.

Sources: Christe C. Armendariz, "A Spy among Us," Password 42, no. 4 (1997): 159–66; Wall, Japanese Texans, pp. 104–105.

Rihei Onishi with daughter May on his lap and his wife, Hisa Nakahata Onishi, left of him, in Webster, Texas, in 1904. Institute of Texan Cultures illustration no. 86-262

Central activities of Buddhist practice in Japan are the chanting and meditating of monks in temples. Most Japanese who came to Texas had been raised as Jodo-shin-shu, or True Pure Land Buddhists, a type of Buddhism that featured repetitive prayers of gratitude leading to rebirth and enlightenment. Japanese also practiced Shintoism. Existing along with Buddhism, Shintoism recognized the divinity found in nature. Japanese offered prayers at small Shinto shrines throughout Japan. Many Japanese blended the two religious traditions as neither tradition claimed to be the only valid one.

Initially, the small number of Japanese in Texas and the distance between their homes made it impossible to recreate Buddhist or Shinto temple worship, but the honoring of ancestors and their inclusion in daily life continued in their homes. Several Japanese leaders had converted to Christianity before coming to Texas, but they also maintained Buddhist or Shinto altars in their homes. Saibara was active in the Webster Presbyterian Church. When his father arrived in Texas, he brought the family scrolls inscribed with generations of family names to ensure that the family's ancestors would accompany Saibara. Kishi, an active Methodist, brought home from a trip to Japan a porcelain statue of the Buddhist goddess of compassion and a scroll listing the family ancestors from his families' home altar. A candleholder, an incense dish, and a vase of fresh flowers were clustered around pictures of his ancestors. The home altar of the Kishis was typical of those that other Japanese placed in their homes, whether or not they attended Christian churches.

The first generation of Japanese Texans sought to adapt to the culture around them. When in public, they dressed like mainstream American citizens. Men wore stylish suits and ties, and women traded their traditional kimonos for the tight-waist, high-neck dresses fashionable in the early 1900s. Workers usually wore loose clothing along with the traditional broad-brimmed hats made of rice straw and

The Onishi farm near Webster, Texas, in 1904. Rihei and Hisa Nakahata Onishi are seated in the doorway with daughter May on her father's lap, ca. 1904. Institute of Texan Cultures illustration no. 86-263

woven straw slippers that were left at the door when entering the house. In private, they continued to follow many customs from their home country.

Traditional Japanese foods made up the diet of early Japanese Texans. The planting of Japanese vegetables such as daikon radishes was among Seito Saibara's first tasks at his new home in Texas. Rice, which they grew, was the staple food in Japan and throughout East Asia. They served rice at every meal; the Japanese word for meal is *gohan,* which means rice. Soybeans were also a vital part of the meals, served as *miso,* a fermented soybean paste; *tofu,* a custardlike soy cake; and *shoga,* a ginger sauce used for flavoring. Often rice and soy products were served with other foods such as *sunomono,* raw vegetables pickled in brine, and cooked seafood served cold. Fish from the Gulf of Mexico replaced those found in Japan. Sometimes it was dipped in *tamari,* soy sauce, or *wasabi,* a hot, green horseradish dressing. Rice cooked in rice vinegar and served with numerous small dishes of vegetables like seaweed and raw or cooked seafood was a Japanese delicacy. Special foods, imported to Texas from Japan or California, included *takuan,* pickled radishes; *nori,* a paperlike, dried seaweed; and *kazunoko,* herring caviar. Hot green tea and *sake,* a Japanese wine, accompanied meals. Sweets included *yokan,* bean cakes, and *mochi,* rice cakes. Rice balls rolled in sesame seeds were another favorite.

Fuji Kishi always served meals to her family and the workers on her fragile blue and white porcelain dishes from Japan. In the Japanese tradition, she arranged the foods artistically in small dishes and placed them around the table. For special occasions, Japanese women placed foods in specially designed lacquered boxes.

Japanese families gathered at holidays for festive celebrations. They celebrated the Asian New Year by preparing traditional Japanese foods and wearing traditional Japanese clothing. The wives prepared *mochi* and *soba,* or buckwheat noodles, which symbolized everyone's desire for a long life, or dumplings, which signified prosperity. In August, the family recognized *O-Bon,* the return of the spirits of the dead. Family members performed folk dances, cleaned cemeteries, and placed offerings of food, flowers, and incense by graves.

Early colonists played *shogi,* a complicated Japanese type of chess, while other family members wrote *haiku,* a seventeen-syllable poem, or *tanka,* a thirty-one-syllable poem: "From all directions / Winds bring petals of cherry / Into the grebe lake."[5]

Dwarf trees, known as *bonsai,* were cultivated, and the women maintained the elegant simplicity of Japanese flower arranging known as *ikebana.* Japanese women also passed down the intricate tea ceremony ritual that emphasized perfection in each gentle movement involved in preparing the tea.

The martial arts were another tradition that was continued in Texas. The Japanese were masters of many defensive systems from *karate,* meaning empty hand, which emerged on the island of Okinawa when weapons were banned, to *jujitsu,* or gentle art, another martial art form that uses opponents' own movements and energy as weapons against them. On the Kishi farm, children also learned Japanese folk songs and dances from records played on a phonograph.

At the Kishi colony, the family built a communal bath consisting of a large, deep tub that sat on a brick stove. Sometimes the tub would be moved into the house. Bathers first rinsed and scrubbed all over, then got in the tub and sat down to soak. The hot water came up to the bathers' necks and provided a relaxing bath.

JAPANESE TEXANS AFTER WORLD WAR II

The war years were difficult for the Japanese living in America. Many had lived in this country for decades. Their children had been born here and it was the only home they knew.

The surprise bombing of Pearl Harbor, Hawaii, was devastating to Japanese Texans. Issei, who had never been allowed to become citizens, were treated hatefully, as if they were personally responsible for their homeland's decision to go to war against the United States. The rights of American citizenship were denied to their children, the Nisei, even though they were citizens by birth. The reaction

Evacuation of Japanese residents from the West Coast in 1943. Institute of Texan Cultures illustration no. 86-255

of citizens to the entry of Japan into World War II following the bombing of Pearl Harbor was rampant hysteria and hatred toward all Japanese Americans in this county. They automatically lost their constitutional rights to due process of law and to challenge evidence of guilt.

In Texas as elsewhere, F.B.I. agents entered Japanese homes, arresting men and taking cameras, short-wave radios, maps, guns, and telescopes to use as evidence that the Japanese Texans might be spies. Sometimes agents harassed family members. When the F.B.I. entered the home of Fukutaro and Ju Akagi near Shelton, Texas, they ransacked the house and destroyed the Buddhist altar where the family honored the dead and said daily prayers. Fukutaro, age 63 at the time, was imprisoned. In addition to what was taken from them by the F.B.I., many families destroyed documents written in Japanese, fearing they would be used as evidence of treason. Neighbors refused them service in stores and spoke harshly against them. However, no one produced evidence that Japanese Texans had ever been disloyal to the United States.

In Texas, many Issei men were arrested and held for lengths of time varying from weeks to years. Women and children remained in their homes, taking care of farms and businesses when the men were imprisoned. Non-Japanese neighbors were sometimes able to secure the release of Japanese men by vouching for their loyalty. The neighbors of Fukutaro Akagi gained his release. A state agency, the Texas Alien Property Custodian, took control of the property of Japanese-owned firms. Nonetheless, some Japanese farmers continued to do well selling the vegetables they had grown in the Rio Grande Valley and near Fort Bliss in El Paso.

The Immigration and Naturalization Service (INS) ran internment camps in Texas, where Japanese Americans were held. The three Texas internment camps were located at Kenedy, Crystal City, and Seagoville. Most of the Japanese Texans were kept at the camp for single men located at Kenedy. These men worked as cheap laborers for local farmers. Others interned at the Crystal City and Seagoville camps included Japanese language teachers from the

The day after Pearl Harbor, these Japanese met with civil and military leaders in San Antonio and pledged their loyalty to the United States. Their pledges did not prevent F.B.I. investigations or arrests. Institute of Texan Cultures illustration no. 2867-C

West Coast and Japanese living in Peru and other South American nations.

In addition to their internment, Japanese businesspeople in Texas often chose or were forced to remove "Japanese" from their businesses. In Houston the Japanese Cafe, begun by Tom Brown Okasaki decades earlier, became Kay's Cafe. Kimi Jingu had created the Japanese Tea Garden from a rock quarry in Brackenridge Park in San Antonio. He and his family had lived in the garden and taken care of it for years. After Pearl Harbor, the Jingus were evicted from the garden. It was renamed the "Chinese Tea Garden" and later the "Sunken Gardens."

Yet Japanese Texans remained loyal to the United States. During World War II, Kiyoaki Saibara, son of Seito Saibara, recorded a message in Japanese, which the U.S. government broadcast by short-wave radio in Japan: "In closing, may I state that we resident Japanese of Texas have accepted the teachings of democracy, and have come to

During World War II the internment camp for Japanese Americans at Kenedy, Texas, was run by the U.S. Immigration and Naturalization Service. Institute of Texan Cultures illustration no. 79-359

The internment camp for Japanese women identified as "enemy aliens" was located at Seagoville, Texas. Institute of Texan cultures illustration n. 85-910

love our country as our own. We are grateful for all the opportunities given us. Our sons and daughters have grown up to be good Americans. Therefore, it is not only our duty but our pleasure to be able to serve this country in this crisis with all the resources at our command, including sending our loved ones into the armed services."[6]

Despite their harsh treatment, some Nisei wanted to fight for the United States in World War II. Initially, they were refused. Then, in January, 1943, an all-Nisei unit, the 442nd Regimental Combat Brigade, was created. Many Nisei volunteered to serve in it. Some Japanese still held in the internment camps joined to regain their freedom and to prove their loyalty to the United States. The 442nd Regiment served honorably in Europe. After fighting in Italy, they were sent to France. When the 36th Texas National Guard unit was caught behind German lines, the Nisei soldiers fought and rescued the "Lost Battalion." In the sixteen days of heavy fighting, many Nisei lost their lives, including Saburo Tanamachi, who had grown up in the Rio Grande Valley. Other Japanese served in the Pacific, where their knowledge of the Japanese language was critical.

Following World War II, U.S. military forces were stationed in Japan. Some of the soldiers married Japanese women who were

Isamu Taniguchi

Isamu Taniguchi was born in Japan in 1887 and immigrated to California when he was seventeen. Starting as an agricultural laborer, he returned to his native village to marry and then returned to California with his wife, Sadayo, to start a farm of his own on leased land. The family was successful and able to purchase land to start a truck farm near Stockton, California. Taniguchi helped create a cooperative for Japanese and Anglo farmers to pack, process, and sell their vegetables.

Shortly after the war broke out with Japan, F.B.I. agents visited the Taniguchi family and arrested Isamu because he was a community leader. After time in the Stockton County jail and various internment camps, he was sent to the camp in Crystal City, Texas. His wife

Ayako Hosaka was the prom queen at Federal High School in the internment camp at Crystal City, Texas. Taken from a page in the Roundup 1945 Yearbook. Institute of Texan Cultures illustration no. 86-317

allowed to accompany them back to the United States. Japanese men in Texas had outnumbered Japanese women four hundred to ten in 1910, but by 1960 there were forty times more Japanese women than Japanese men in Texas, with the vast majority married to non-Japanese military men. The military brides had little in common

and younger son were also arrested and were reunited with Isamu at Crystal City. The Taniguchis lost all their property in California. After release from the Crystal City camp, Taniguchi started farming in the Rio Grande Valley where he worked successfully until the age of eighty.

Taniguchi's older son had been in school at the University of California, Berkeley, before his internment at a different camp from his family. Originally named Yamato, he took the name Alan hoping to gain acceptance. When he obtained his release from the camp, he worked as a draftsman. He became an architect in the Rio Grande Valley and, ultimately, the dean of architecture at the University of Texas in Austin. He created a monument to the Japanese American

The Jingu family created and managed the Japanese Tea Garden in San Antonio for over two decades before being evicted during World War II. Institute of Texan Cultures illustration no. 84-348

Shigeru Imai, top row, third from left, of Aldine-Westfield, Texas, with fellow members of the 442nd Regiment Combat Team and their girlfriends, ca. 1944. Institute of Texan Cultures illustration no. 79-321

internees at Crystal City.

When Isamu Taniguchi retired and moved to Austin, he wanted to contribute to world peace. His pet project became the creation of the Oriental Garden at Zilker Park in Austin. Working alone for eighteen months, he turned three acres of cliffs into a beautiful space. Grafting cherry blossoms onto wild plum trees, he reproduced the beauty and harmony of a traditional Japanese garden. As Isamu explained it, "The garden is the embodiment of the peaceful coexistence of all the elements of nature." Isamu Taniguchi died in 1992, having given Texans the gift of a place of peacefulness.

Source: Isamu Taniguchi, Massey research files from *Fascinating Texans Project* (San Antonio: Institute of Texan Cultures Library, 1995).

The military funeral at Arlington National Cemetery in Washington, D.C., of Saburo Tanamachi, a Nisei soldier from Texas, who was among those killed rescuing the soldiers of the Texas National Guard Unit from behind German lines in 1943. Institute of Texan Cultures illustration no. 86-338

with the Japanese Texans who had arrived earlier. The young women created their own clubs and social groups. In El Paso they organized their own Buddhist group, a branch of the Soka Gakkai International, popular in Japan after World War II. Members met in each other's homes and practiced repetitive chanting.

In 1952 the Issei, Japanese Americans who had originally emigrated from Japan, were finally allowed to become U.S. citizens. Many Japanese Texans gladly took advantage of this right. Postwar economic growth in Texas also allowed Nisei, the second generation of Japanese Texans, to move into professional jobs. Many Issei and Nisei in the internment camps did not want to return to the West Coast after the war, and some of them settled in Texas, greatly increasing the numbers of Japanese Texans.

Isamu Taniguchi stands in the Japanese Peace Garden that he created for the pleasure of Austin citizens. Institute of Texan Cultures illustration no. 96-418

Following World War II, there were deep and bitter feelings in Japan against Americans as a result of Hiroshima and Nagasaki. As Japan rebuilt its economy, few Japanese were interested in immigrating to the United States. Over the decades, the number of Japanese Texans has held steady with 28,060 living in Texas as of the 2000 census.

CHAPTER 3

Filipino Texans

THE 7,100 PHILIPPINE ISLANDS, lying off the coast of Southeast Asia, are home to people whose ancestors came from many cultures, some native to the various island tribal groups and some descendants of traders and conquerors who arrived from Asia, Europe, North America, and the Middle East. The Chinese occupied the islands for over three hundred years, followed by Arab and Indian traders, the Spanish, and lastly the Americans. The years of Spanish rule established Roman Catholicism as the religion of most Filipinos. Occupation by the United States throughout the first half of the twentieth century exposed Filipinos to the English language and to the lifestyle of those serving in the U.S. military. The major islands are Mindanao, Luzon, and Visayas. Over seventy-five language groups are spoken among the islanders, but in 1946 they adopted Tagalog as the national language.

In 1521, Magellan, a Portuguese explorer sailing for Spain, reached the islands where he died in battle. Captain Juan Sebastián del Cano continued Magellan's voyage around the world and brought word to Spanish royalty of the Philippine Islands. Galleons and ships sailed carrying trade goods between Manila and Acapulco in New Spain from 1565 to 1815. The islands were a major trading center with Manila as the main port. The first Filipino to settle in Texas was a sailor who left the islands on a Spanish cargo ship in 1822 at the age of thirteen.

Others came to Texas in the early 1900s as students or with the military families who had employed them in the Philippines. With

> **Francisco Flores**
> *Francisco Flores was born in the central Philippines about 1809. At age thirteen, he left his home island to be a cabin boy on a large Spanish schooner. As a sailor, he traveled around the world, watching as the captain and crew transported slaves from Africa to the United States. Saving his money, he bought two large schooners that he used to fish and trade along the Gulf Coast. At age forty he married and settled in the small village of Rockport.*
>
> *Francisco and his eldest son, Agapito, worked the fishing trade together until Flores retired to live with his daughter Josefina and enjoy his grandchildren. His younger son, nicknamed Manila, fought in World War I. Francisco Flores died at age 108 in 1917, and many*

passage of the Philippine Independence Act in 1934, the United States stopped Filipino migration as the islands began to prepare for independence that was to occur after a ten-year transition period.

World War II brought increased opportunities for Filipino immigration. Philippine scouts, initially assigned to assist the United States in its conquest of the islands around 1900, again fought side by side with U.S. forces against Japan in World War II. Together they faced defeat, hunger, and death. On July 4, 1946, the United States granted the Filipinos their independence.

Some Filipinos who had fought alongside U.S. military troops received citizenship and joined the U.S. military. Fort Sam Houston became the home of former Filipino scouts, creating a Filipino community in San Antonio. Among the scouts was Alfredo Quijano, the son of a Filipino scout who had fought with the U.S. Army in 1900. During World War II, Alfredo and his father were captured by the Japanese and then released. After his release and recuperation, Alfredo joined the U.S. military forces. He became a U.S. citizen before ever coming to America. While serving in the army, he married and started a family. In 1949 he came to the United States. Three years later his wife and children followed. The family remained in San Antonio where they had several more children.

Other cities with military bases also began to develop significant Filipino populations. In addition, numerous Filipinas were among the war brides that came to Texas.

With the reform of the immigration laws in 1965, the number of Filipino Texans increased dramatically. Educated in U.S. schools in the Philippines, they often had the professional and technical training desired by American industries. The jobs in the expanding fields of medicine and engineering in Texas combined with a coastal climate much like their home country's attracted Filipinos to the state. Medical schools in the Philippines had a strong tradition of excellence, and medical practices, public health services, and nursing in Texas particularly profited from the skilled work of Filipino Texans.

Instead of the young single men who had come before World War II, the migrants who came to the United States after 1965 were primarily Filipino women and families. According to the new law, once one family member became a citizen, other family members could come. As more and more came to the state, centers of Filipino population shifted from San Antonio and El Paso to Houston. Only about four hundred Filipinos were in Texas in 1950, but by 2000 there were 75,226 Filipino Texans.

In major cities around the state, a wide range of Filipino societies and organizations developed including Filipino branches of national organizations, various Filipino business and medical associations, senior centers, and social clubs. Many of the organizations helped Filipinos become established in Texas business and society. Filipinos also have taken the lead in encouraging Asian Americans to become involved in politics. Organizations devoted to preserving the arts and customs of the Philippines also emerged.

of his descendants still reside in Texas.

Source: Letter by Mrs. Conrad Compnest, "Biography of the First Filipino in Texas," Mar., 1979, "Filipinos," vertical file, Institute of Texan Cultures, San Antonio, Texas.

THE CULTURE OF THE FILIPINO TEXANS

Many cultures contributed to the traditions of Filipinos. Some of the islands retained the Malaysian traditions of particular tribes, while the Chinese and Spanish influenced others. The southern islands were strongly Muslim, a fact that was reflected in their traditional dances and dress. Most Filipinos were Roman Catholics, as were most Filipino Texans, although there were some Filipino Protestant churches in the state. Many different tribal languages were spoken in the Philippines, but those immigrating to Texas usually arrived fluent in English.

Festivals in large Texas cities provided Filipinos with a chance to enjoy their shared heritage, to teach customs to their children, and to introduce their culture to other Texans. The independence of the Philippines from 377 years of Spanish rule in 1898 is celebrated annually on June 12 with dinners and other festivities. In Euless, Texas, Filipinos gather for an all-day celebration with regional foods and native dress. Children play games that their parents and grandparents played while growing up in the Philippines. The Fourth of July (1946)

In 1974 the Filipino American Association of San Antonio held a Philippine festival at La Villita that included a traditional hut. Institute of Texan Cultures illustration no. 75-1214e

is celebrated both as an American holiday and as the day the Philippines gained its independence from the United States.

In the Philippines, each Catholic village had its own patron saint with annual festivals following the calendar of the Roman Catholic Church. Some of the festivals continued in Texas. Christmas brought a lantern parade, while Easter was celebrated with the Salubong in which a group of women met a group of men coming from the opposite direction, symbolizing the meeting of Jesus with his mother after the Resurrection. All Saints' Day was observed with the cleaning of graves. In January Filipinos commemorate the Feast of Santo Niño. When Cebu Island Queen Juana converted to Christianity in 1521, Magellan presented her with a statue of the child Jesus. A few years later when another Spanish expedition arrived in 1565, battles broke out with the local people. In the rubble following the battle, fires ignited a box containing the statue, which was unharmed. Many miracles are attributed to the powers of the image, and the Feast of Santo Niño is held by Filipinos throughout the world.

The Flores de Mayo, or Flowers of May, honors the Virgin Mary, and the Santa Cruzan marks the discovery of the holy cross. These two popular festivals are celebrated together. Pageants present the history of the church, and a queen of the celebration is crowned. Participants perform distinctive dances and wear clothing representing different areas of the Philippines.

Native dances were a favorite part of the Filipino culture and were performed regularly at festivals in Texas. Dance groups were organized among local young people, and dancers from the Philippines frequently visited the state. Some dances came from particular islands or regions of the country and depicted Malayan, Arabic, or Spanish influences. Some portrayed events in the life of a village, such as harvesting, hunting, fighting, courtship, or death. Others

Filipino dancers pose in traditional dress before a performance at the Institute of Texan Cultures. Institute of Texan Cultures illustration frame no. 15

displayed natural elements such as wind and rain or birds and animals or tell folktales through dance.

Traditional Philippine clothes were worn at the different festivals and dance performances. Various islands had their unique tribal costumes. Originally worn on formal occasions by elite women, the traditional Santa Maria dress, with its long, flowing skirt, butterfly sleeves, and elaborate hand-embroidered decoration had been adapted but was still worn by Filipinas on special occasions. Traditional dress for men was the *barong tagalog,* an elaborately embroidered shirt worn with its tail over men's long wrapped skirts. When the Spanish forbade Filipinos from tucking in the shirttail when wearing suits with coats, they started wearing the colorful shirts to formal events.

In the traditional Filipino culture, there are many beliefs about good luck. If someone wears polka-dot clothing at the beginning of the year, prosperity is likely for the remainder of the year. The blessed coins thrown at a baby christening also bring good luck to the person who catches one. Filipinos also believe that bad luck arises from putting your arms or hands behind your head.

Each of the major islands also has different food preferences. The food habits of Filipino Texans depend on the island that was home, but there is a common emphasis on chicken and pork in dishes like *pansit,* a favorite noodle dish, and *lumpia,* or egg rolls.

The martial arts of the Philippines are reflective of the many Filipino cultures. When the Spanish arrived, they declared the martial arts forbidden. Not to be deterred, the Filipinos devised ritual and cultural "dances" that were actually fighting-art training sessions. When bladed weapons were declared illegal, Filipinos switched to hardwood sticks, and stick fighting became an advanced martial art skill unseen in other Asian cultures.

The degree to which the customs and traditions of the homeland are maintained by Filipino Texans depends, in part, upon the closeness of continued ties to the islands and the continued existence of family and relatives there.

CHAPTER 4

Korean Texans

KOREAN TEXANS come from a small peninsula south of China and west of Japan. For much of its history, Korea has fought to maintain its independence and cultural identity against invasions from its powerful neighbors. Although the Chinese had exerted a strong influence in the late nineteenth century, Japan gradually increased its power over Korea.

During this time, many Koreans left and worked as laborers in the sugar fields of Hawaii, with a few moving on to the United States. Joshua Lee came as a laborer from Korea to work in the Hawaiian sugar fields. He selected his picture bride, Angeline, from a series of photographs of Korean women and then sent money for her to come to Hawaii where he married her. During the Depression, Joshua left Hawaii and went to a college in Indiana where he earned an engineering degree. He returned to Hawaii and got a job harvesting sugar. He worked his way up in the company, eventually becoming a vice president. His daughter Wendy also came to the United States to go to school. After getting her degree, she worked as an economics professor at Texas A&M University where she met her future husband. Wendy Lee is a Korean Texan married to ex–U.S. senator Phil Gramm.

When Japan conquered Korea and made it part of its empire in 1910, all Koreans were prohibited from leaving. Christian missionaries tried to aid the Koreans in their opposition to the Japanese occupation. After World War II, both the United States and Russia sought to control Korea. The country was divided in half, and in

Joshua Lee and his picture bride, Angeline, with their three children. Institute of Texan Cultures illustration no. G-220

1950, when war between North and South Korea broke out, each side received aid from foreign supporters. Some Koreans left their homeland and went to South America. With U.S. troops stationed in Korea, marriages took place between the soldiers and local women. Korean War brides came to the United States when their spouses returned home. In Texas, the couples often settled in El Paso, San Antonio, Killeen, and other towns with military bases.

Open immigration laws after 1965 allowed more Koreans to immigrate. Like other recent immigrants, they were drawn to Texas by jobs in medicine, science, and education. Some held technical and skilled jobs in the oil industry. Korean nurses came in particularly large numbers. When the economy slowed in the 1980s, many Koreans lost high-paying jobs and opened shops, which they and their families ran. Today, Korean shops, offering goods and services to other Koreans, are frequently clustered together, near other Asian businesses, making it easier for new arrivals that do not know English to shop. Other Korean businesses sell clothes, electronics, and items in African American and Mexican neighborhoods. Koreans have also entered the wholesaling business, selling large quantities of goods to stores throughout Texas cities.

Another group of Korean Texans arrived in the state in the 1990s and set up small shops in Eagle Pass, Laredo, Brownsville, and other towns along the Mexican border. In El Paso they dominated the area south of downtown where the Chinese had shops a century earlier. With connections to Korean industries, they obtained Korean-made goods, which they then sold cheaply to the Mexican people along the Rio Grande. Some arrived with money to start their shops, while others pooled their money in traditional Korean organizations called *gyes* or *kyes.* More Koreans presently own small businesses in Texas than any other ethnic group. For example, Ho Yun Lee had migrated from Korea to Paraguay where he stayed for thirteen years before eventually moving to Virginia. He was in Virginia for two years and then came to live and open a shop in El Paso.

Like other Asians, Koreans practice a blend of religious traditions. The oldest, animism, recognizes and honors spirits found in

Sarah Kielty of Austin, Texas, celebrates her first 100 days' birthday, following Korean custom. Institute of Texan Cultures illustration no. 101-318

nature. Confucian thought adds respect for social order, education, and close, hierarchical family ties. Buddhism emphasizes rituals, chants, and a compassion for all living creatures. Today, many Korean Texans worship at the Buddhist temples in Houston and Dallas.

In the late nineteenth century, Christian missionaries entered Korea, and many Koreans converted to various Protestant denominations. Some Korean Texans were Christians in their homeland.

Many more joined Korean Christian churches after their arrival in Texas. Koreans have generally formed their own congregations. Churches create a place where Koreans can meet and form close bonds with other Koreans. Small church-related groups make up for the fact that Korean Texans do not live together in one neighborhood or community. Arriving primarily as wives and as families, Koreans find community at their churches and shops.

Like other Asians, Koreans celebrate the New Year with such traditions as housecleaning, payment of debts, and welcoming of ancestors. Traditional foods include *duk,* or rice cakes, that are shaped into logs, sliced, and served in chicken or pork broth. Another dish might be *mandoo,* which is a dumpling stuffed with meat or vegetables. Sweets such as *yak bap* are also made from rice and included in most New Year's celebrations.

Korean food is popular in Texas, and there are numerous Korean restaurants in various cities. The most widely known Korean food is *kimchi,* a form of spicy sauerkraut served as a condiment with other foods and eaten daily by many Koreans. There are many varieties of *kimchi.* Making big batches of it is sometimes a family or neighborhood ritual, but it is a smelly project. The cabbage is pickled for a month in a sauce made with daikon radishes, lots of garlic, and fine, red hot pepper. Additional vegetables or seafood are sometimes added. Another favorite food is known as Korean barbecue, or *bulgogi,* a thinly sliced beef marinated in a blend of sesame seed oil, soy sauce, onions, and garlic. In El Paso, Korean cafes sell Mexican foods alongside Asian foods. Sometimes cafes blend the traditions. Teh Chom Kang serves tacos, burritos, and hamburgers as well as Chinese dishes like almond chicken, but his specialties are Korean *bokum bap,* fried rice, with *ojingo bokum,* fried octopus.

Korean dances growing out of Buddhist, farmer, and court traditions are still performed. Distinctive Korean musical instruments include drums, gongs, harps, and pipes. Colorful native costumes include full, high-waisted dresses worn with long, puffed-sleeved jackets for women. Men wear full pants and long coats or short jackets.

The practice of the martial art of tae kwon do is another way in which Koreans continue their traditions. Tae kwon do emphasizes kicking techniques, and while there are over thirty other Korean martial art systems, it is the most prevalent one. It has recently become an Olympic medal sport, and tae kwon do is now one of the most popular martial art forms in the world. By balancing mind, body, and spirit, the martial arts foster self-discipline and courtesy.

The lives of many Texans are enriched by the cultural gifts of the over fifty thousand Korean Texans.

CHAPTER 5

Indian and Pakistani Texans

INDIA BECAME an independent nation in 1947, and Pakistan was created as a separate country at that time. Previously, Great Britain had ruled the total region as a colony for almost two hundred years, leaving its mark on education, language, and lifestyle, especially among the elite of India.

India is one of the most multicultural countries in the world with society divided by more than six hundred languages as well as by religion, geographic region, and the remains of the caste system. Diverse regional and religious identities remain strong with major differences existing between northern and southern Indians. Although the formation of Pakistan as an Islamic nation was intended to lessen religious tension and violence, no such positive results have occurred, and violence between and within the countries continues.

Prior to 1924 very few immigrants from India came to the United States because of the laws prohibiting Asian immigration. Indian Sikhs, members of a religious group started five hundred years ago in northwestern India who taught tolerance of other faiths, came as farm laborers in small numbers to California around 1900, but it was not until immigration restrictions changed in 1965 that immigrants of the elite class from India and Pakistan began entering Texas.

Indian men and women who were educated in English-speaking schools and colleges moved quickly into high-paying jobs in Texas. They worked in industrial, educational, and medical centers as scientists, engineers, managers, and college faculty. Doctors and nurses also came in large numbers. They could earn more than they had earned at home and often more than other Texans. Men brought wives and children with them or returned to India to marry. Women often held professional jobs while maintaining their families and homes according to Indian domestic traditions. One scholar has claimed that these initial immigrants "may be the most talented and easily acculturated of all immigrants in the long history of American immigration."[1]

The slowdown of the Texas economy in the 1980s and the arrival of more varied immigrants from India and Pakistan resulted in a broader range of employment and incomes. Some immigrants from Pakistan and India own retail stores, investment services, banks, motels, convenience stores, and other businesses. In Del Rio, merchants from India have specialized in selling gold and expensive jewelry to buyers from Mexico.

Most Indians and Pakistanis have entered Texas recently, their numbers increasing significantly with each census. In 2000 there were 142,689 people from India, making them the second largest group of Asian Texans. If the additional 25,324 Pakistanis in Texas were combined with the Indians, their numbers would exceed those of the Vietnamese, the largest Asian group in Texas. Most of the immigrants have settled in Houston and Dallas, but significant clusters live in Austin, Lubbock, College Station, San Antonio, Waco, and Midland-Odessa, where they often work as physicians or other professionals.

Even though Indians and Pakistanis adapted quickly to life in the state, they still enjoy the company of others who share their language and culture. They relish Indian social and cultural events. The Indian and Pakistani cultural centers provide them with native dance, music, films, and festivals. In Houston they gather regularly to play cricket, a game of British origin. While western dress is normal at work, social events prescribe that Indian women wear the traditional *saris*, the draped clothing of India. Some also wear *bindi*, a dot on the forehead that traditionally signified that a woman was married. Today it is worn by unmarried girls and all women except for widows.

Bana Ramanath

Bana Ramanath was born in her grandmother's home in a village in southern India. As a child, she often returned to the village, which contained thousand-year-old temples, to spend summers.

Because her father was a high-ranking government official, Bana grew up in Bombay and frequently moved to other cities in India. Her talents led her into athletics and dance. She traveled throughout India as a cross-country runner. When teachers from the Kalakshetra Dance School observed her dancing, she was invited to study at a leading school of classical Indian dance. While dancing she also attended college, starting at the early age of fifteen.

Immigrating to the United States as the wife of a medical student, Bana Ramanath lived in Detroit and El Paso

Bana Ramanath is a dancer who learned the classical dances of India before coming to Texas. Institute of Texan Cultures illustration no. 101-328

before moving to San Antonio in the 1980s. She had given up dance performances because her husband's conservative traditional family in India had disapproved. After arriving in San Antonio, she began to dance again and to accept students interested in learning classical dance. Her first classes were held in her kitchen and then in her garage.

As her dance classes gained in popularity, Bana created the Natyanjali and Natya Dance Institutes in San Antonio and Austin. She returns to India regularly and stays in contact with dancers and musicians there. She is a devout Hindu and values the many cultures of India. She is an articulate cultural ambassador, interpreting India's many traditions and beliefs for fellow Texans.

Source: Bana Ramanath, oral history interview by Sara Massey, 2001, Institute of Texan Cultures, San Antonio, Texas.

Indians and Pakistani parents care deeply about their children's education and success. Conflicts between American and Indian values, such as parents not wanting their children to date at a young age, sometimes emerge between parents and children. Arranged marriages were traditional in India, and while the rules are loosening, parents often expect to be involved in choosing whom their sons and daughters will marry.

Air travel, E-mail, and wealth have made it easier for Asian Indians to remain in contact with their families back home. They visit India regularly and send children to spend time with their grandparents who can immerse them in Indian culture.

Parents are particularly concerned that their children learn to appreciate and maintain their particular religious and regional traditions. Religion remains one of the strongest ways in which Indian

Young girls in a dance recital demonstrating traditional classic dances of India at the Institute of Texan Cultures. Courtesy of Sarah Massey

and Pakistani culture is passed on. Almost all immigrants from Pakistan are Muslims. The majority of immigrants from India are Hindu, with significant minorities of Muslims, Sikhs, Jains, and Parsis/Zoroastrians also present. Even within Hinduism, great diversity exists. Although Buddhism began in India, few Indians are followers.

At the heart of Hinduism is an assumption that the divine is both one and many, beyond all understanding and embodied in nature. The statues of gods and goddesses in both temples and private homes express what Hindus consider ultimately inexpressible. Stylized images of deities reveal different aspects of the divine and portray religious stories, allowing worshippers to grasp religious truths by sight rather than by words. For Hindus, the mind and body are one, and practices like yoga teach "one-pointedness," or the ability for total concentration. *Puja,* or devotion, involves bringing flowers, incense, food, and other gifts as offerings to the gods and goddesses. Reading of sacred texts and meditation are also performed. Family rituals are observed daily, and most families have shrines and images in their homes.

Hindus place little importance on religious congregations, in contrast to most Christians. Temples often have separate shrines for several gods and goddesses. They are built in traditional ways by craftsmen from India and represent the Hindu cosmos. Festivals bring a variety of Hindus together to honor divinity or special events in Hindu religious history and myth. At least thirty-four Hindu temples and religious centers exist in Texas, with about fifteen in Houston and the Dallas–Fort Worth Metroplex area.

Most Hindu groups in Texas started with a few students or families gathering to worship, sing, or study together. Gradually, larger groups emerged and built temples. The range of temples reflects the variety within Hinduism, as some retain a regional focus while others seek to bring together many different Hindus. In Houston, for example, the Sri Meenakshi Temple is modeled after a temple to a goddess in Madurai, India. The temple's rituals reproduce traditional religious activities for Indians. Another temple in Houston

Ganesha, a Hindu God who is a remover of obstacles. Institute of Texan Cultures illustration

focuses on Hindu thought and language, and a Hare Krishna temple is dedicated to the worship of the god Krishna with the repeated chanting of his name. Other temples have formed around particular Hindu leaders.

Hindus may have a primary commitment to a particular temple and tradition, but lines between groups blur. Hindus often participate in festivals held by any group of Indians. The Dallas/Fort Worth Temple Society has sought to bring together Hindus from various practices. Temples have secular activity as well as religious services. They offer after-school classes and summer camps for children to learn the languages and religious practices of India. Adults also gather for study, lectures, and to enjoy each other's company. Some groups draw non-Asians into their circle.

Festivals occur throughout the year, drawing hundreds of people. Hindus celebrate Diwali, the New Year Festival of Lights, Holi in the spring, and the Chariot Festival with a procession carrying the god's image. With a Hindu population of forty thousand in Houston in the 1990s, a citywide gathering of six to ten thousand members of the Indian community celebrated the birthday of the god Krishna at the convention center.

A graphic illustration of a Hindu temple located in Helotes, Texas. Courtesy of Sarah Massey

Hindu families mark various points in people's lives with rituals such as the name-giving rite for babies. Held at a temple, this is traditionally the first excursion out of the home for a new mother and the baby. Teenage boys celebrate a rite of passage in which they eat a special meal prepared by their mothers and then go before their teacher, or guru.

Virtually all immigrants from Pakistan and a significant minority from India are Muslims, the followers of the Islamic religion. In the eleventh century, the Muslim Empire spread from Spain and Africa through India to the Pacific islands that now compose Indonesia and the Philippines. Some people in these nations have retained their commitment to Islam. The tradition makes particular effort to exhibit tolerance for people of different races and cultures within Islam and Muslims from all over the globe, making it attractive to blacks whose African ancestors had embraced the tradition.

At the center of the Islamic faith is the often-repeated belief that "there is no God but Allah, and Muhammad is the Prophet of God." Muslims seek to live their lives in submission to Allah, who is compassionate and merciful to those who obey his will. Allah's words are recorded in the Qur'an (Koran) to be read, heard, and followed by all Muslims. The Qur'an was revealed to Muhammad, an Arab living in what is now Saudi Arabia in the sixth century after the birth of Jesus in the Christian religion.

Muslims follow the Five Pillars of Islam: belief, prayer, fasting, almsgiving, and pilgrimage:

Belief that Allah, as revealed by Muhammad, is loving and in total control.

Prayer five times a day, facing Mecca, the site in Saudi Arabia where Muhammad first experienced Allah's revelations.

Fasting during the month of Ramadan, by not eating or drinking during the hours of daylight.

Almsgiving to those who are poor and oppressed is expected and helps to equalize wealth among Muslims.

Making a pilgrimage to Mecca during their lifetime if they are able.

Muslims live and worship throughout Texas. Muslims from Pakistan, India, and other Asian nations have immigrated here in recent decades. Over three dozen mosques and Islamic centers have been created in Texas plus even more urban storefronts where Muslims gather for prayer. According to one Muslim in Houston, "No matter where you are in Houston, there is always someplace close by where you can go to pray."[2] Mosques are places where Muslims gather for Friday afternoon prayer services and talks.

Because Muslims come from many countries and traditions, Muslims in Texas represent and continue a variety of cultural traditions. For example, Muslim women from the Middle East typically wear a scarf, or *hijab,* draped around their head out of modesty. Muslim women from Pakistan are much more likely than those from Arabic countries to dress the same as other Texas women.

Some of the Muslim rules do not fit easily into non-Muslim workplaces and schools. Consequently, some Texas school districts have arranged to accommodate the needs of Muslim students for their required daily prayers during school hours and on Fridays. Muslims also have strict rules about modesty and ask that their children, especially their daughters, not participate in physical education classes and activities. In addition, Muslims do not eat pork and have special requirements about cleanliness. Because of the difficulties in getting schools to accommodate Muslim practices, some parents have created private Muslim schools for their children.

Indian food is much more diverse than the typical Indian restaurant menu. The majority of Indian restaurants serve various meat dishes from northern India. Many of the people coming to Texas from western India are vegetarians. Spices are important in all Indian cuisines, but they vary from region to region and from family to family.

Many immigrants from India and Pakistan arrived with the skills and resources to succeed in professions, businesses, and schools in Texas. This success in America has not diminished their desire to pass on their diverse religious and cultural traditions. Their presence has added yet another dimension to the rich diversity of the Texas people.

CHAPTER 6
Vietnamese Texans

THE VIETNAM WAR of the 1960s and 1970s marked another significant turning point in the arrival of Asians in the United States and Texas. As war spread over the Indochina peninsula, refugees from Vietnam, Cambodia, and Laos were driven from their homelands by war and personal danger, often leaving with nothing but the clothes they wore. Many carried the scars of war. Their escapes from their homelands, including witnessing the death of family members and friends, hunger and thirst endured over long uncertain days at sea in flimsy boats, and extended stays in refugee camps, were traumatic. Unlike other Asian Texans, they came because they had to escape their countries, not because they dreamed of coming to the United States. Many had never considered leaving their homeland and could not imagine living in Texas, a place few knew even existed. A Vietnamese tells about his continuing sorrow:

> On the outside, I am like an American. I drive to work in my car. I eat hamburgers at lunch. But on the inside, I am Vietnamese; I cannot forget my mother, hungry in Vietnam, while I have it easy here.
>
> Although they are deeply grateful for the basic freedoms of America, they feel in but not of this culture, yet there is no homeland to which they can return. They realize that they represent the end of an era, a way of life that will never again be seen. . . .
>
> It is a tremendous upheaval of not only history and culture, but also the emotional conquests and bitter griefs of a people. It is the anguish in a heart that feels the departure of the soul, but still has

> the strength in spirit to struggle for survival. It is the endless tale of the lives of Vietnamese people, who have the courage to suffer . . . and continue to live with what fate has dealt them.[1]

The Indochina peninsula, where Vietnam, Cambodia, and Laos are located, is home to diverse ethnic groups. Small tribal kingdoms had once ruled there, but fighting among the countries and with neighboring China disrupted their development as a nation. The whole area became French colonies in the late 1800s. French rule contributed little in Laos and Cambodia; schools, railroads, and cities

Vietnamese family arriving at the San Antonio airport. The Vietnamese women are wearing traditional ao dai, *dresses with high collars, long sleeves, and slits on the side.* Institute of Texan Cultures illustration no. En4-10-82, frame 8A

were seldom built. Most people lived in simple, isolated farming villages. In the Vietnamese lowlands, however, the French language, Roman Catholicism, and French education created a local elite. During World War II, Japan occupied Indochina. After the war, the nationalists in Vietnam began demands for independence. War broke out in Vietnam between the French who wanted to reestablish their authority and the nationalists and communists who sought home rule for the country. When the French were beaten, the United States stepped in to fight the North Vietnamese. The United States sent increasing numbers of military forces into the region.

When Saigon, the capital city of South Vietnam, fell to the North Vietnamese in 1975, local people who had aided the United States feared for their lives. As U.S. troops withdrew, vast numbers of Vietnamese left with them. Most of this "first wave" went to refugee camps in nearby countries. They were then transferred to relocation centers where their education about life in the United States began. Locations where refugees were placed were scattered throughout the United States in order to keep large numbers from dominating any region. Working with the government, churches, and other organizations, individual Texas families agreed to sponsor Vietnamese immigrants. As sponsors, the families were to provide for housing and food, help the immigrants to find jobs, and assist them in learning how to function in the new culture. Problems emerged due to lack of planning and the fact that some sponsors were more interested in cheap labor than in offering support.

Among the first wave of people were educated and well-to-do individuals and families who knew some English, had professional training, and were accustomed to working with U.S. citizens. By 1977 a second wave of refugees left Vietnam, Laos, and Cambodia. In Vietnam the establishment of strict communist rule had made life difficult and food scarce. Chinese, who had dominated the economic community in Vietnam, had their businesses taken over by the government and were sent to primitive camps. Escape was dangerous. Vietnamese escaped in overcrowded boats that often sank, killing many aboard before they could reach safety. These "boat

Mymy Tran

Mymy Tran was born in Vietnam and came to America as a refugee at fifteen. She escaped Vietnam with her father and two brothers as part of the wave of boat people. Their transport boat was stopped in the Philippines, where they were held in a refugee camp for eighteen months until a sponsor in North Carolina volunteered to help them. Her mother and other sisters remained behind in Vietnam and did not come to this country until sixteen years later.

In North Carolina, Mymy went to college at North Carolina State where she earned a degree in engineering. She married Dang Tran, a Vietnamese man who had immigrated to Seattle where he had gone to school. He obtained work with IBM and was

people" gave vivid accounts of being robbed and beaten by pirates and losing family members during the voyage.

Once in America not all Vietnamese found acceptance or satisfaction with their communities. Many were isolated from other Vietnamese and were very lonely. They desired the familiarity of people from their own culture who spoke their language. They also sought the presence of other Asians so that they could have traditional foods and make money selling Asian goods and services. Accustomed to the warmth of their homeland, those sent to the northern part of the United States fared badly in the cold. Gradually, large communities of Vietnamese refugees congregated in a few locations. One of the largest of these was in Houston, second only to Los Angeles in the size of its Indochinese population.

Houston and the Texas Gulf Coast offered a climate much like that back home. Men traditionally skilled in running boats and fishing on the open sea in Vietnam were drawn to the Gulf Coast. In turn, the presence of a large Vietnamese community became a magnet drawing others to settle in the region.

The second wave of Vietnamese refugees in Texas faced enormous problems. The majority did not speak English and could not read in any language. The only life most knew was that of rural farm villages. Some refugees had never used refrigerators, stoves, or modern bathrooms. Bartering and growing vegetables in the garden was not an option now, and they had to learn how to shop for food in grocery stores. In addition, these were people still suffering the emotional traumas of war, the loss of loved ones, and dislocation.

The employment process for most Vietnamese was also very difficult. Even those Vietnamese with education and professional experience found themselves initially employed in low-paying, unskilled jobs. Men trained as physicians in Vietnam had to go through the long process of retraining and certification before they could practice medicine in Texas. Once licensed, they sometimes took jobs in small Texas towns such as Avery, Hale Center, Cooper, and Detroit where the rural Texans who had not had local medical care in years welcomed them.

Mymy and Dang Tran at her naturalization ceremony in San Antonio, ca. 1998.
Institute of Texan Cultures illustration no. G-204-34

transferred to North Carolina where he met Mymy. They were married in 1994 and then he was transferred again—to Austin, Texas.

In 1998 Mymy became a naturalized citizen in Texas, and now works for an Austin company.

Source: Mymy Tran, *New Texan* interview by Mary Grace Ketner, 1997, Institute of Texan Cultures, San Antonio, Texas.

Vietnamese who knew a little English sometimes found jobs as sales clerks outside their neighborhood. Those who spoke only Vietnamese owned and worked in shops in their own community that sold products like fresh lotus root, rice paper, fish sauce, and books written in Vietnamese. Trade schools taught welding and carpentry, which helped some to get jobs in shipyards or on construction projects. Other Indochinese found jobs in factories or as laborers, while some worked as janitors and servants. Not all refugees, however, were able to earn more than the minimum wage.

Although plagued by low-paying jobs, many Vietnamese made gains through the strong work ethic that has traditionally been a part of the Vietnamese culture. Many refugees were willing to work long hours and endure poor conditions to get ahead. Rejecting government aid whenever possible, large families crowded into tiny

Learning the English language was a priority for Vietnamese refugees. Institute of Texan Cultures illustration no. En 12-8-75, frame 10

rooms to save money. Frequently they used meager earnings to purchase homes or to start small businesses with all family members from children to grandparents contributing their unpaid labor.

Yet this valuable work ethic sometimes caused problems. Violence erupted between the Vietnamese who moved into the shrimp and fish industry along the Gulf Coast and the men who had been there for generations. Unable to speak English, the Vietnamese fished as they had in their homeland. Intent on doing well, they fished day and night, often breaking established local customs. When they saw a fisherman succeeding, they brought their boats up close to share in the good luck, not realizing that in Texas fishing was a very individualistic pursuit.

Violence erupted in the coastal community of Seadrift in August, 1979, when several Vietnamese boats were burned, and a vacant

Vietnamese learn to use American supermarkets rather than growing produce in village gardens. Institute of Texan Cultures illustration no. En 5-26-75

Vietnamese home was firebombed. A fight between white and Vietnamese fishermen ended with the fatal shooting of a white crabber. Eventually peace was established, and the Vietnamese accused of murder were acquitted. Efforts at communication between the two groups of fisherman began. The laws and the customs of Texas fishing were written down and translated into Vietnamese.

Finding good places to live also created problems for Vietnamese. Sponsors provided initial housing for the refugees, but it seldom fit their traditional ways of living. The extended families and the many children did not fit into the small dwellings or apartments available for low rent. Their cooking, incense, and noise sometimes bothered those who lived nearby. In addition, the Vietnamese took screens off windows to dry fish and spread their fishing nets out in the yard. They were accustomed to raising and butchering pigs and chickens and growing vegetables in their yards. They had no experience at keeping a lawn mowed to look pretty.

The poverty-stricken areas where the Indochinese often lived presented other problems such as crime. Not used to trusting police, the Vietnamese suffered. As soon as they could, some Vietnamese bought larger dwellings in the suburbs. Others settled near each other, filling apartment complexes and recreating villagelike surroundings. For example, Sinh Tran, once a military officer who had escaped from a "reeducation camp" in Vietnam, served as a leader for refugees in an apartment complex in Houston much as he might have done in a village in his homeland. Stressing communal responsibility, he remarked, "Within these four walls, I would do anything for you, and you would do anything for me."[2]

Some Vietnamese youth who had grown up in the chaos of refugee camps had little reason to respect any type of authority. They formed gangs and demanded money from other Vietnamese who they knew were afraid to report their actions to police.

Like other immigrants, the Vietnamese created organizations such as mutual aid societies to help new arrivals find housing, jobs, and learn the skills needed to survive in a new setting. Some Vietnamese tutored children struggling to learn English in order to suc-

A Vietnamese Texan family at home in San Antonio. Institute of Texan Cultures illustration no. En10-4-79, frame 4A

ceed in the public school system. They organized Boy Scouts and Girl Scouts within their communities. Young women learned traditional Vietnamese dances, while the elderly gathered for conversation in their own language. Job-counseling programs assisted those seeking work. Vietnamese orphans, including those children fathered by American soldiers whose mothers were Vietnamese women, received special attention. Vietnamese who had received aid when they first arrived in Texas felt a duty to be there for others in need.

The Vietnamese retained a strong sense of obligation to family left behind and feared for their safety. As Kim Thoan Tran said, his "feelings of sadness in leaving my family and my country were so strong. My wife and daughters came with me, but as for the rest, they were left behind."[3] In addition, some, especially those who once served in the government or army, continue to dream of returning to their homeland and ousting the communists. Some Vietnamese still hold informal gatherings each year to observe the fall of Saigon.

During decades of French rule, many Vietnamese had adopted Roman Catholicism, and the Catholic Mass became one of the few familiar aspects of their new life in Texas. Catholic churches and organizations did much to aid the refugees. Vietnamese priests and nuns who were among the refugees took leadership roles in establishing Vietnamese communities and churches. Catholic churches, such as Saint Peter's Indochinese Mission Church in Rockport, were built to serve the Vietnamese community. Among the refugees were a group of Vietnamese Carmelite nuns who learned English in hopes of better serving other refugees. In south Houston they taught English along with Vietnamese songs and dances to Vietnamese children.

Other Vietnamese retained their traditional Buddhist practices. Gradually, Buddhist temples appeared around the state, following the Mahayana tradition of Buddhism also present in China and Japan. Some temples and their grounds, like the Vietnamese Buddhist Temple in Houston, were created to resemble those the Vietnamese had known in their homeland. Grounds included ponds, lotus flowers, and statues of Buddha and other figures from the Buddhist tradition. Inside the temple stood large statues of Buddha and low cushions on which worshippers are seated. Monks are less remote from the people than they had been in their native country and more likely to explain Buddhist practices. A gong signals the entrance of monks and the beginning of worship, which includes chants, reading of *sutra,* the sacred writings of Buddhism, and words from a monk. At the temples, the presence of other Vietnamese and the

A Vietnamese Texan family forms its own family orchestra. Institute of Texan Cultures illustration no. En5-11-84, frame 7

use of their own language help lessen the shock of Texas society. Although Buddhism does not require attendance at a weekly service, worshiping at the temples anchors refugees in their own spiritual traditions.

Buddhist Vietnamese usually have small shrines in their homes with a figure of Buddha and pictures of their ancestors. Fruits and other offerings are left on these shrines. Sometimes monks advise on their placement of objects and bless them. At these shrines, Vietnamese may also observe the death day of family members and ancestors. They may write messages to ancestors on red slips of paper that are burned on the altars. These home shrines also play a role in Vietnamese Buddhist marriage ceremonies. In-laws meet and accept each other into their families at the home shrines of both the bride and groom. If parents remain in Vietnam, this part of the ceremony is videotaped and exchanged.

In Port Arthur the Queen of Vietnamese Martyrs Catholic Church stands near the Buu Mon Buddhist Temple. On the Peace Plaza between them is a statue of the Virgin Mary standing on a globe. Many Vietnamese live within walking distance, allowing family elders to worship when they choose. Businesses serving the Vietnamese are nearby. Although some Texans worry about the growth of Vietnamese ghettos, living and worshiping together provides support for refugees who often have to leave the community for work and school.

Tet, the Vietnamese Lunar New Year celebration, unites Vietnamese regardless of their religious practices. Tet is a time of feasting, merrymaking, and gift giving. Food is offered to honor ancestors with or without belief in their actual presence. Efforts are made to ensure good luck in the coming year. Before Tet, everything is made clean, bright, and shiny with flowers placed everywhere. At midnight on the last day of the year, or Giao Thua, people go to temples amid the ringing bells and beating drums. They return home bearing branches from temple gardens. For the next three to ten days, they engage in activities such as games and martial arts. There are traditional songs and dances with performers wearing ornate costumes. Young women dance with candles, hats, fans, and scarves. A dancing dragon or lion, with martial artists forming the body and legs and a large papier-mâché head, moves and jumps with the drumming. The lion dance recalls a legend in which a lion saved a village from a monster, thus driving away evil and bringing good luck. Traditional foods such as seed candy, roasted watermelon seeds, coconut, and ginger-root cookies are cooked and served.

Other festivals punctuate the Vietnamese year. Trung Thu, an autumn festival, features children dressed in traditional clothes with paper lanterns moving around the temple grounds. Moon cakes are served, and celebrations include singing traditional songs and dancing with the paper lions and dragons. An affirmation of piety takes place in July or August with crowds of people honoring their ances-

Lion dancers prepare to perform at a celebration. Institute of Texan Cultures illustration no. En3-18-83, frame 17A

tors and praying for the redemption of their sins. Those within the Buddhist tradition also celebrate Buddha's birth and enlightenment. Other holidays honor national Vietnamese heroes.

The Vietnamese are proud of their heritage and appreciate the presence of other Vietnamese in Texas. They eat their traditional foods, buying them in Asian shops or growing them in home gardens. The Chinese influence in Vietnam is reflected in their foods. The methods of cooking such as boiling, steaming, frying, and baking, along with the seasoning used, make the food uniquely Vietnamese. Vietnamese egg rolls are made with a thin rice paper, while Chinese egg rolls are made with wheat-based wonton skins. Rice, a food staple, is served with Asian vegetables such as bitter melon, water spinach, taro root, winter melon, garlic chives, daikon radishes, Japanese eggplant, and long beans. Cumin, basil, and mint are often added. Women have traditionally done the gardening and continue to raise these vegetables when land is available. Although their gardens tend to be small, women often sell excess produce to Asian groceries and restaurants as a means of earning money.

French colonization also left influences on Vietnamese cooking such as the use of leeks, garlic, and shallots. Crisp salads of lettuce, cilantro, and cucumbers are often served alongside fried foods like spring rolls. Vietnamese restaurants appeared in Texas in the late 1970s. The numerous beef dishes and salads have become popular with many Texans.

The immigration experience of the Vietnamese has been a difficult one. Leaving not by choice but by necessity and abandoning all, many Vietnamese immigrants suffered unthinkable trauma. Many are also still mourning loved ones left behind in Vietnam. In addition, their arrival in a country divided by the Vietnam War did not lead to a warm reception or sympathetic understanding of their plight. As the years have passed, Vietnamese Texans have learned the English language and made adjustments to their surroundings. In the 2000 census, they accounted for the largest Asian group in Texas, at 143,352 strong.

CHAPTER 7

Cambodian and Laotian Texans

AS THE SECOND WAVE of Vietnamese refugees escaped communist rule, war had spread to the rest of the Indochina peninsula. U.S. bombing raids into Cambodia in the early years of the war had caused great destruction there, and a procommunist force known as the Khmer Rouge gained control of the country, renaming it Kampuchea. Their leader, Pol Pot, was intent on destroying all Cambodians who had been influenced by American and European ideas. One of the world's most enormous bloodbaths ensued, and most of the country's educated people were killed. The entire population was turned out of Cambodia's major cities and marched through the countryside. The Khmer Rouge executed massive numbers of teachers, doctors, and other professionals. Simply wearing glasses was enough to condemn a person to death as an "intellectual." Revenge against tribal groups in the mountainous regions was also vicious. Disease and starvation added to the death toll. When other communists invaded Cambodia from Vietnam, the chaotic conditions allowed refugees to attempt escapes, but their stories were grim. For example, one young girl who came to Austin had witnessed the death of her friend and lost her own eye after stepping on a land mine near their work camp. Her eye had become infected, but there were no doctors to treat it.

Laos also suffered from American bombing and from the advance of communist forces. The Pathet Lao used the support of the North Vietnamese to dominate the country. Families, the basic social unit in the country, were split up and sent to government work

Cambodian women of Texas sewing together in a social group. Institute of Texan Cultures illustration no. En1982-11-6, frame 19

camps where many died of overwork and hunger. Warfare between communist and noncommunist forces became widespread. Especially hard hit were tribal groups in the mountains of Laos, such as the Hmong, who had provided services to the U.S. military. When possible, refugees from Laos escaped across the border into Thailand, where the language and culture were similar to their own.

Almost all Laotians arriving in America came after the 1975 communist takeover of the country. They had few skills for dealing with American society. Cambodians and Laotians have had an especially difficult time making a place for themselves in Texas society. Isolation in rural villages had kept them from exposure to other cultures and languages and modern society. Their homelands, among the poorest in the world, had been devastated by warfare. Widespread killing in both countries left those who did escape burdened with guilt and grief. Both Cambodians and Laotian groups regard Vietnamese as their traditional enemies and strongly dislike being mistaken for them.

Theravadian Buddhism, which differs from the Buddhism practiced in Vietnam and other Far Eastern countries, is practiced in both Laos and Cambodia. This Buddhism is strongly influenced by the folk practices of the region. Laotians celebrate their New Year, Pi Mai, in April. In addition to cleaning their homes to get rid of bad spirits, they wash the statue of the Buddha and sometimes pour water on each other. Cambodians also greet the year with Chaul Chhnam Tmey, an event during which they spend three days visiting family and friends and performing religious ceremonies.

Laotians and Cambodians in this country have found strength in creating places where they can live together as they did in their homelands. For Laotians, the village and the Buddhist temple, the Wat, require each other's existence. In Laos, Buddhism focused on temples and monks. Most people practiced their religion by "earning merit," usually by giving food and other gifts to monks. In return, the monks chanted and meditated, taught the children, healed the sick, and counseled the people of the village. Temple rites in a village honored their shared ancestors.

By creating their own village and Wat in North Texas, some Laotians have found a center for their lives. Monks, who were not allowed to earn a living or even cook, came from Thailand to start the community and build the Wat. Laotians and Thai who had clustered in the Dallas–Fort Worth area were eager for a temple that practiced Theravadian Buddhism. They contributed generously to the construction of the new Wat. People from throughout the area came for monthly celebrations. Evening chants and meditation generally drew the women and elderly from within the community. The women are thought to represent the whole family so that other members do not need to attend.

Cambodians also have chosen to live in groups. Some settled in Breckenridge and near Mineral Wells at the former military base of Fort Wolters. In Austin a former military man heads the family clan, and in Houston many have clustered in the same apartment complexes. Although shopping and services are available in nearby Vietnamese neighborhoods, work and school ensure that some members of the community interact with the larger society.

Laotians, like many mountain-dwelling people, use herbs and fewer spices in their cooking than do other Asian cultures. Many of the herbs as yet do not have English names, but lemongrass, Asian basil, and lemon basil are now available in many stores run by Asians.

Arriving in large numbers, Indochinese refugees from Cambodia and Laos have faced bigger obstacles than other Asian immigrants have in making a home for themselves in Texas. In the process, the 8,225 Cambodians and the 11,626 Laotians living in Texas in 2000 brought their traditional religion and culture, which for many of them has contributed to their survival.

Conclusion

Increasing numbers of Asians are becoming part of the population of Texas. Census totals clearly reflect that the changes in the immigration laws of 1965 had a profound effect on increasing the immigration of numerous Asian ethnic groups to the United States.

During the 1990s more than 257,000 Asians and Pacific islanders immigrated to Texas. They comprised 2.7 percent of the state's population, ranking Texas fourth in total Asian American population—behind California, New York, and Hawaii. Almost half of all Asian Texans live in the Houston area.[1] By the 2000 census there were 657,664 Asians in Texas. While some decided to discard the culture and religion of their native lands, others found identity and peace in continuing familiar customs and assembling with others who shared their language and traditions. Participating in traditional practices affirmed their past while easing their adjustment to

TABLE 3
U.S. Census Totals for Asian Texans

	1890	1920	1940	1970	2000
Chinese	710	773	1,031	7,606	112,950
Japanese	3	449	458	8,388	28,060
Filipino		30	219	4,999	75,226
Korean		4		2,102	54,300
Asian Indian				2,014	142,689
Pakistani				161	21,324
Vietnamese					143,352

Source: U.S. Bureau of the Census, "Population 1890–1990" (Washington, D.C.: Government Printing Office); www.census.gov/main/www/cen2000.html

jobs, homes, and life in Texas. A college student, majoring in business, described his changed attitude about his Vietnamese identity:

> In high school, I had more American friends. I was totally American. . . . I thought that in order for you to succeed, you needed to be American. . . .
>
> At times I did not see myself as being any color. I hang around with whites; I thought I was white. It never hit me that I was yellow. . . . I prided myself on being able to bridge the gap between Vietnamese and American. I think it is part of the hogwash that Americans teach you in grade school. . . . I bought into that for a few years, and in high school, I had conflicts with Vietnamese because I thought they were not putting themselves forward and accepting the Americans. . . .
>
> I think after college and my experience here, what I see happening, I don't think it is their fault. There is racism in America. . . .
>
> When you get into a corporation, no matter how smart you are, if you are Vietnamese or Oriental, you won't go very far, so you are just fooling yourself. . . .
>
> I can be 100% assimilated but I choose not to be. Maybe 20% or 30% American and 80% or 70% Vietnamese. . . . The price of assimilation is losing your identity and if you are willing to pay for it and it doesn't hurt you, that's fine. But if you don't choose to assimilate, there is also a price you have to pay.[2]

Asians have experienced hostility from other Texans in the past and continue to do so into the present. Despite their growing numbers and their importance in the state, Asians are generally ignored and rendered invisible unless events force them to the attention of their fellow Texans. The East Coast terrorist attacks of September 11, 2001, were such events. Using bricks and rocks, some individuals broke the windows of mosques and homes in half a dozen Texas cities. Sikhs and Hindus were assumed to be Muslims and harassed by those who could not distinguish between South Asian and Middle Eastern peoples. A man from Pakistan was killed while working at his convenience store in Dallas. He was not robbed, and presumably hatred and anger at Asians motivated the murder. He was working hard to make his shop a success before allowing his wife and children to join him in Texas. Relatives said that he had come to America because he thought that the United States would be a safer place to live than Pakistan.

If nothing is known of our Asian neighbors, then their differences can be threatening. Ignorance breeds mistrust. Most Muslims worship the same God of love as Christians, despite the fact that terrorists use their religion to justify their destructive acts. Learning about the customs and values of our Asian neighbors, as they are learning about our diverse practices, can bring us closer together. By talking with them about their traditions and by attending their celebrations and festivals, we can learn to appreciate the rich and varied cultures of Texas. We can share our identity as Texans at the same time we honor our ethnic differences.

Notes

CHAPTER 1. CHINESE TEXANS

1. *San Antonio Daily Express,* Oct. 16, 1882.
2. Ibid.
3. *El Paso Herald,* Jan. 11, 1904.
4. Jim Eng, oral history interview by Laurie Gudzikowski, May 20, 1997, Institute of Texan Cultures, San Antonio, Texas.
5. Amy Elizabeth Nims, "Chinese Life in San Antonio" (master's thesis, Southwest Texas Teachers College, 1941), pp. 16–17.
6. *El Paso Herald,* Feb. 11, 1904.
7. Grace Tin-Ling Chen, "Double Happiness," *Houston Post Magazine,* Dec. 4, 1988, vertical file, Institute of Texan Cultures, San Antonio, Texas.

CHAPTER 2. JAPANESE TEXANS

1. African Americans and their descendants received citizenship after the Civil War. During the 1800s a few Asians were granted citizenship. As more Asians arrived, however, rulings that they were not white and thus could not become citizens ended the hope of becoming citizens.
2. Lillie Mae Tomlinson, "The Japanese Colony in Orange County," *History Teachers' Bulletin* 14 (University of Texas Bulletin Series, 1927): 141.
3. "Family Told to Move On," *Austin American,* Jan. 7, 1921.
4. "Declares Japs are No Menace," *El Paso Herald* 14, no. 5, Mar. 14, 1921, pp. 5–6, quoted in Christie Celia Armendariz, "Inconspicuous but Estimable Immigrants: Japanese in El Paso, 1890–1948" (master's thesis, University of Texas at El Paso, 1994).
5. "History of Haiku," http://www.asd.k12.ak.us/schools/romig/asia2/Culture/Haiku/main.html (Jan., 2002).
6. Thomas Wall, *Japanese Texans* (San Antonio: Institute of Texan Cultures, 1987), p. 166.

CHAPTER 5. INDIAN AND PAKISTANI TEXANS

1. Raymond Brady Williams, *Religions of Immigrants from India and Pakistan: New Threads in the American Tapestry* (Cambridge: Cambridge University Press, 1988), p. 21.

2. Quoted by Hoda Badr, "Al-Noor Mosque: Strength Through Unity," in *Religion and New Immigrants,* Helen Rose Baugh and Janet Saltzman Chafez, eds. (Walnut Creek, Calif.: Alta Mira Press, 2000), p. 195.

CHAPTER 6. VIETNAMESE TEXANS

1. Bich Naga Hoang (Ann Hoang), "Vietnamese Texans: Refugee Settlement in Texas," research for the Institute of Texan Cultures, 1989–90, pp. 70–71, 80, copy in vertical file, Institute of Texan Cultures, San Antonio, Texas.
2. *Houston Chronicle,* Dec. 29, 1996.
3. Hoang, "Vietnamese Texans," p. 44.

CONCLUSION

1. Randy Mallory, "Asian Cultural Festivals," *Texas Highways,* Feb., 2002, pp. 12–19.
2. Interview with Vinh, twenty-two-year-old male student at University of Texas at Austin, quoted in Huong Hoai Tran, "Assimilation of Vietnamese Refugees in the United States" (master's thesis, University of Texas at Austin, 1990), pp. 66–69.

Bibliography

County histories and the manuscript census were valuable in following the Chinese through the small towns of Far West Texas. Vertical files from the Institute of Texan Cultures were also useful. Websites were an important source of information about various religions in Texas. Most were accessed through http://www.pluralism.org produced by the Committee on the Study of Religion at Harvard University.

Barkan, Elliott. *And Still They Come: Immigrants and American Society, 1920s to the 1990s.* Wheeling, Ill.: Harlan Davidson, 1996.

Baugh, Helen. *Religion and New Immigrants.* Walnut Creek, Calif.: Alta Mira Press, 2000.

Bhookong, Sadhon. "A Laotian Refugee Community: Its Impact on Adaptation." Ph.D. diss., Texas Woman's University, 1990.

Briggs, Alton. "The Archeology of 1882 Labor Camps on the Southern Pacific Railroad in Val Verde County." Master's thesis, University of Texas at Austin, 1974.

Briscoe, Edward Eugene. "Pershing's Chinese Refugees: An Odyssey of the Southwest." Master's thesis, Saint Mary's University, San Antonio, 1947.

Chan, Sucheng. *Asian Americans: An Interpretive History.* Boston: Twayne Publishers, 1991.

Chen, Edward C. M., and Frank von der Mehden. "The Chinese." In *The Ethnic Groups of Houston,* ed. Frank von der Mehden, 63–79. Houston: Rice University Studies, 1984.

Clarke, Joan. *Family Traditions in Hawaii.* Honolulu: Namkoong Publishing, 1994.

Daniels, Rodger. *Coming to America: A History of Immigration and Ethnicity in American Life.* N.Y.: Harper Collins, 1990.

Eck, Diana L. *A New Religious America: How a "Christian Country" Has Now Become the World's Most Religiously Diverse Nation.* San Francisco: Harper San Francisco, 2001.

Farrar, Nancy. "The History of the Chinese in El Paso, Texas." Master's thesis, University of Texas at El Paso, 1970.

Field, William. *Chinese Texans.* San Antonio: Institute of Texan Cultures, 1981.

Ganeri, Anita. *Religions Explained: A Beginner's Guide to World Faiths.* N.Y.: Henry Holt, 1997. (Juvenile)

Glasrud, Bruce. "Asians in Texas: An Overview, 1870–1990." *East Texas Historical Journal* 39, no. 2 (2001): 10–22.

Glenn, Evelyn Nakona. *Issei, Nisei, War Bride: Three Generations of Japanese American Women in Domestic Service.* Philadelphia: Temple University Press, 1986.

Kwon, Hyonchu. "Entrepreneurial Activities and Religious Behavior among Korean Immigrants in the Houston Area." Master's thesis, University of Houston, 1994.

McGee, Lorrie A. "No Direction Home: Cambodian Refugees Coming of Age in America." Master's thesis, University of Texas at Austin, 1989.

McMurray, David Andrew. "The Austin Cambodian Refugee Community: A Study in Social Dynamics." Master's thesis, University of Texas at Austin, 1982.

Melendy, H. Brett. *Asians in America: Filipinos, Korean, and East Indian.* Boston: Twayne Publishers, 1977.
Nakano, Mei. *Japanese American Women: Three Generations, 1890–1990.* Berkeley: Mina Press Publishing with the Japanese American Historical Society, 1990.
Nims, Amy. "Chinese Life in San Antonio." Master's thesis, Southwest Teachers College, San Marcos, 1941.
Ochiai, Hisako. "The Community of the Japanese Americans in the Rio Grande Valley." Master's thesis, Texas A&I University, 1974.
Pido, Antonio. *The Pilipinos* [sic] *in America: Macro/Micro Dimensions of Immigration and Integration.* N.Y.: Center for Migration Studies, 1986.
Reimers, David. *Still the Golden Door: The Third World Comes to America.* 2d ed. N.Y.: Columbia, 1992.
Rhoades, Edward J. M. "The Chinese in Texas." *Southwestern Historical Quarterly* 81 (1977): 1–36.
Spickard, Paul R. *Japanese Americans: The Formation and Transformations of an Ethnic Group.* N.Y.: Twayne Publishers, 1996.
Staksi, Edward. *Beneath the Border City: The Overseas Chinese in El Paso.* Las Cruces: New Mexico State University, University Museum, 1984. Occasional papers. #13.
Takaki, Ronald. *Strangers from a Different Shore: A History of Asian Americans.* N.Y.: Penguin Books, 1989.
Thernstrum, Stephen, ed. *Harvard Encyclopedia of American Ethnic Groups.* Cambridge, Mass.: Belknap Press of Harvard University, 1980.
Tomlinson, Lillie Mae. "The Japanese Colony in Orange County." *History Teachers' Bulletin* 14 (University of Texas Bulletin Series, 1927): 141–45.
U.S. Immigration Commission. Part 24, "Recent Immigrants in Agriculture." Chapter 7, "Japanese Rice Planters and Truckers in Texas," 463–81. Washington, D.C.: Government Printing Office, 1911. 61st Cong., 3d sess., S. Doc. 633. "Dillingham Report."
Ueda, Reed. *Postwar Immigrant America: A Social History.* Boston: Bedford Books of St. Martin's Press, 1994.
von der Mehden, Frank. "The Japanese." In *The Ethnic Groups of Houston,* ed. Frank von der Mehden, 101–12. Houston: Rice University Studies, 1984.
———. "The Indochinese." In *The Ethnic Groups of Houston,* ed. Frank von der Mehden, 82–99. Houston: Rice University, 1984.
Wall, Thomas. *The Japanese Texans.* San Antonio: Institute of Texas Cultures, 1987.
Williams, Raymond Brady. *Religions of Immigrants from India and Pakistan.* Cambridge: Cambridge University Press, 1988.
Wingate, Gwendolyn. "The Kishi Colony." In *The Folklore of Texan Cultures,* ed. Frances Edward Abernathy, 323–33. Austin: Encino Press, 1974.
Zepp, Ira. *A Muslim Primer: A Beginner's Guide to Islam.* Westminster, Md.: Wakefield Editions, 1992.

Index

ISBN 1-58544-312-3
90000
9 781585 443123